A
FLUMMERY
of
FOOD

Les Garçons, by Aubrey Beardsley

A
FLUMMERY
of
FOOD

FEASTS
for
EPICURES

ANDRÉ SIMON

First published in the United Kingdom in 2004 by Little Books Ltd,
48 Catherine Place, London SW1E 6HL.

10 9 8 7 6 5 4 3 2 1

A CIP catalogue record for this book is available from the British Library.

ISBN: 1 904435 44 0

The author and publisher will be grateful for any information that will assist them
in keeping future editions up-to-date. Although all reasonable care has been taken in
the preparation of this book, neither the publisher, editors nor the author
can accept any liability for any consequences arising from the use thereof, or the
information contained therein.

Many thanks to: Debbie Clement for jacket design and layout conception,
Jamie Ambrose for editorial production and management,
Claudia Dowell for editing,
Mousemat Design Limited for production consulting and management.
Printed and bound by Scotprint in Scotland.

Contents

There is no one who does not eat and drink. But few there are who can appreciate taste.

CONFUCIUS

INTRODUCTION

Gastronomy is the hallmark and the most rewarding achievement of our Western civilization. Sheer self-gratification is all that the gluttons and hedonists care for; not so the gastronomes. They are the fortunate people who were granted at birth the use of all their senses and the rarer gift of common sense to use them rightly, all of them: the senses of taste and smell as much as sight and hearing.

Some of us, we know, are born blind and others are born deaf; and there are those who are born tone-deaf or colour-blind, and they never can be artists nor singers. Likewise those who do not happen to be born with normal senses of taste and smell can never be gastronomes, but this does not mean that they never will be famous. The great Duke of Wellington, for instance, could never tell beef from mutton: he had no taste-buds, in spite of which he certainly did quite well in life; he did miss a great deal, nevertheless, as all must who take no interest in their daily meals.

Gastronomes do take an interest, an intelligent and pleasurable interest, in their meals. Food is not just fuel to them, but fun as well.

Their senses of taste and smell have been trained by constant practice and they have become highly sensitive, which means that they will readily appreciate and inwardly enjoy the right balance and pleasing harmony of well-cooked food partnered with suitable wines; but, naturally, it also means that they may only too often be made painfully aware of gastronomical heresies or shortcomings which do not offend others, just as anybody with an ear for music winces at a flat note which goes unnoticed by others.

Practice makes perfect, and the pianist who is a gastronome as well as a good musician, as Mark Hambourg was and as most pianists are, does not grudge the time he has to spend every day at practice, and still less the time which he spends at table, and not by himself this time.

Gastronomes may be greedy up to a point, but they never are gluttons; they know too well that there never can be any real appreciation where there is excess, and that without self-control the golden rule of moderation in all things has no meaning. Gastronomes do not make a god of their belly; they make it their servant, a servant well-deserving of every consideration, since it is responsible for the 'good conduct' of all the inner works upon which their bodily health and good temper depend to such an extent.

In gastronomy, as in all arts, the amateur can be as good as the professional; and, like all artists, gastronomes can make others share their experiences by recounting in the right manner either pleasurable occasions or lamentable disappointments in the field of gastronomy. A number of gastronomes among gifted writers of all times and many nations have recorded their views on most matters of gastronomic interest, and the selection of their writings which has been assembled in these pages will be enjoyed by all who appreciate good writing as well as good fare and good wine.

ANDRÉ L. SIMON

'It's a naïve domestic Burgundy without any breeding,
but I think you'll be amazed by its presumption.'

(Drawing by James Thurber; © 1937, *New Yorker Magazine* Inc.)

TO INDULGE OR
NOT TO INDULGE

Tell me what kind of food you eat, and
I will tell you what kind of man you are.

BRILLAT-SAVARIN

THE SALMI OF LIFE
(What the Soul of the Young Man said to the Waiter)

Tell me not in figures wavy
That my bill is twelve-and-nine,
When I had but soup of gravy,
Steak, potatoes, cheese, and wine.

I'm a poet, I'm a rhymer,
Hardly versed in traders' tricks,
But a pint of *Laubenheimer*
Ought not to be four-and-six.

Though I'm not at all unwilling
To assist you to success,
I must say I think a shilling
Far too much for watercress.

Bills are long, and cash is fleeting,
And I wish to make it clear
That the bill you are receipting
Is the last I settle here.

When you've fleeced your guests and fined them,
I may venture to explain,
They will shake the dust behind them,
And they won't come back again.

So I leave you, poorer, sadder,
Lest you make me poorer still;
Sharper than the biting adder
Is the adder of the bill.

ADRIAN ROSS

A HYMNE TO BACCHUS

Bacchus, let me drink no more:
Wild are the seas, that want a shore.
When our drinking has no stint,
There is no one pleasure in't.
I have drank up for to please
Thee, that great cup of Hercules:
Urge no more; and there shall be
Daffadills g'en up to thee.

ROBERT HERRICK

THE REASON WHY

Those predisposed to epicurism are for the most part of middling height. They are broad-faced and have bright eyes, small forehead, short nose, fleshy lips and rounded chin. The women are plump, chubby, pretty rather than beautiful, with a slight tendency to fullness of figure.

It is under such an exterior that we must look for agreeable guests. They accept all that is offered to them, eat without hurry, and taste with discrimination. They never make any haste to get away from houses where they have been well-treated, but stay for the evening, because they know all the games and other after-dinner amusements.

Those, on the contrary, to whom nature has denied an aptitude for the enjoyments of taste are long-faced, long-nosed, and long-eyed; whatever their stature, they have something lanky about them. They have dark, lanky hair, and are never in good condition. It was one of them who invented trousers.

BRILLAT-SAVARIN
Gastronomy as a Fine Art (1826)

THE
Accomplished LADY's
Delight in Cookery;
OR, THE
Complete Servant's-Maid's
GUIDE.

WOLVERHAMPTON: Printed by J. SMART.

The Accomplished Lady's Delight in Cookery ; or, the Complete Servant's – Maid's Guide. Illustrated title page showing a woman preparing food, and people around a table. J. Smart; Wolverhampton, c.1780

A cartoon by Henri Toulouse-Lautrec, artist and gourmet

Importance of Minding One's Belly

Some people have a foolish way of not minding, or of pretending not to mind, what they eat. For my part, I mind my belly very studiously and very carefully; for I look upon it that he who does not mind his belly will hardly mind anything else.

Samuel Johnson

The Wholesome Dyet

The wholesome dyet that breeds good sanguine juyce, such as pullets, capons, sucking veal, beef not above three years old, a draught of morning milk fasting from the cow; grapes, raysons, and figs be good before meat; Rice with Almond Milk, birds of the Field, Feasants and Partridges, and fishes of stony rivers, Hen eggs potcht, and such like.

Nicholas Breton
Fantastickes, Serving for a Perpetual Prognostication (1626)

Eating and Old Age

A series of strictly exact observations has demonstrated that a succulent, delicate and choice diet delays for a long time and keeps aloof the external appearances of old age. It gives more brilliancy to the eye, more freshness to the skin, more support to the muscles; and as it is certain in physiology that it is the depression of the muscles that causes wrinkles, these formidable enemies of beauty (to which may be added 'flabbiness' and 'fleshiness'). It is equally true that, all things being equal, those who know how to eat are comparatively ten years younger than those ignorant of that science.

BRILLAT-SAVARIN
Gastronomy as a Fine Art (1826)

Digestion is the great secret of life.

SYDNEY SMITH

Before Drinking

Drinke first a good large draught of Sallet Oyle, for that will floate upon the wine which you shall drinke, and suppresse the spirites from ascending into the braine. Also what quantitie soeuer of newe milke you drinke first you may well drinke thrise as much wine after, without daunger of being drunke. But howe sicke you shall bee with this preuention, I will not heere determine, neither woulde I haue set downe this experiment, but openly for the helpe of such modest drinkers as sometimes in companie are drawne, or rather forced to pledge in full bolles such quaffing companions as they would be loth to offend, and will require reason at their hands as they terme it.

SIR HUGH PLAT
The Jewell House of Art and Nature (1594)

Plaint of a Perverse Palate

I have dined too long off delicate food:
I am now in far too coarse a mood:
Bring me a thick beefsteak *saignant*,
A mountain of cheese and an onion,
Garlic soup and a smoking mess
Of fish unknown to *bouillabaise*!
My palate is perversely off
Dinde truffé, sauce Strogonoff...
I have drunk too deep of delicate wine
To broach a bottle of Rieselstein,
Hospices de Beaune or Gruaud Larose,
Nuits-St-Georges or any château's
Ancient and throat-caressing *cru*:
I thirst for some far stronger brew.
The fierce and brutal joys I seek
Of Planter's rum from Martinique,
Grappa and vodka and arrack,
Eau de vie and applejack.
I am bored with cocktails at the Ritz:
Bring me a bottle of slivovitz.

GEORGE SLOCOMBE
Wine and Food, 14

VEGETABLE IFS

If Leekes you like, but do their smelle dislike, eat
Onyons, and you shall not smell like Leeke. If you
of Onyons would the scente expelle, eat Garlicke
that shall drowne the Onyon's smell.

Philosophers' Banquet (1633)

AN ALTERNATIVE TO EATING AND DRINKING

It is a frequent solemnity still used with us, when
friends meet, to go to the alehouse or tavern, they
are not sociable otherwise: and if they visit one
another's houses, they must both eat and drink. I
reprehend it not, moderately used; but to some
men nothing can be more offensive; they had
better, I speak it with Saint Ambrose, pour so much
water in their shoes.

ROBERT BURTON
The Anatomy of Melancholy (1621)

THE CURE

Let, then, every man who has drunk too deeply from the cup of pleasure, every man who has devoted to work a considerable part of the time due to sleep, every man of wit who feels that he has temporarily become stupid, every man who finds the air damp, the weather unendurable, or time hanging heavy on his hands, every man tormented with some fixed idea which deprives him of the liberty of thinking — let all such people, we say, prescribe to themselves a good pint of chocolate mixed with amber in the proportion of from sixty to seventy grains to the pound, and they will see wonders.

BRILLAT-SAVARIN
Gastronomy as a Fine Art (1826)

An Eighteenth-century Cure by Claret

Sir John Royds was indebted to claret for his very unexpected recovery; during the last week of the disease they poured down his throat from three to four bottles of that generous beverage every four-and-twenty hours, and with extraordinary effect.

The Memoirs of William Hickey

After Drinking Cure for the Heid-ake

Take green Hemlock that is tender, and put it in your Socks, so that it may lie thinly between them and the Soles of your Feet; shift the Herbs once a Day.

The Hon. Robert Boyle
Medical Experiments (1692-4)

By Any Other Name

When the bill against spirituous liquors was past, the people 'at Norwich, Bristol and other places, as well as at London, made themselves merry on the death of madam gin, and some of both sexes got soundly drunk at her funeral, for which the mob made a formal procession, but committed no outrages. Riots were apprehended in the metropolis, so that "a double guard for some days mounted at Kensington: the guard at St James's and the house Guards at Whitehall were reinforced, and a detachment of the Life Guards and Horse Grenadiers paraded Covent Garden, etc." But there were no disturbances. To evade the Act the brandy shops in High Holborn, St Giles's, Tothill Street, Rosemary Lane, Shore Ditch, the Mint, Kent Street, etc, sold drams under the names of Sangree, Tow-row, Cuckold's Comfort, Parliament Gin, Bob, Make Shift, the Last Shift, the Ladies' Delight, the Balk, King Theodore of Corsica, Cholic, and Grape Waters, etc.'

The London Magazine, October 1736

The Bedroom Companion

The wines were chiefly port, sherry and hock; claret and even Burgundy being then designated 'poor, thin, washy stuff'. A perpetual thirst seemed to come over people, both men and women, as soon as they had tasted their soup; as, from that moment, everybody was taking wine with everybody else till the close of the dinner; and such wine as produced that class of cordiality which frequently wanders into stupefaction. How all this sort of eating and drinking ended was obvious, from the prevalence of gout, and the necessity of everyone making the pill box their constant bedroom companion.

CAPTAIN R H GRONOW

In Defence of Drinking

What do they know of Heaven, Sir,
who only know the stars?
We, too, can reach these heights,
my friend, who sit in public bars,
On gin and on martini, yes, and with lager beer,
We, too, can wander Heavenwards,
our feet in sawdust here.
Add to these, moreover, the bright lights
and the song,
The joy of all the ancient soaks
who suddenly feel strong,
Who feel young blood run through their veins,
who suddenly feel fine.
Do not condemn these blessings, Sir,
when you condemn our wine.

Some think the world twirls on its stem,
because of love, young love.
But some of us have been through that
— and found the going rough.

So whether (lads) we loved and lost,
or if we loved and won —
We still thought all the world was ours when
we were twenty-one.
Love warms the cockles of our heart
— and that's its great design,
But so can good old alcohol, God bless its
swinging sign,
Since when we've been through everything,
from war to What's My Line,
So think upon these horrors, Sir, ere you
condemn our wine.

NANCY SPAIN

There was an Old Person of Hurst,
Who drank when he was not athirst;
When they said, 'You'll grow fatter,'
He answered, 'What matter?'
That globular Person of Hurst.

EDWARD LEAR

A Little Drunkenness Discreetly Used

To unbosom myself frankly and freely to your Grace, I always looked upon Drunkenness to be an unpardonable Crime in a young Fellow, who, without any of the foreign Helps, has Fire enough in his Veins to do Justice to *Coelia* whenever she demands a Tribute from him. In a middle-aged Man, I consider the Bottle as only subservient to the nobler Pleasure of Love; and that he would suffer himself to be so far infatuated by it, as to neglect the Pursuit of a more agreeable Game, I think deserves no Quarter from the Ladies. In old Age, indeed, when it is convenient to forget and steal from ourselves, I am of opinion that a little Drunkenness, discreetly used, may as well contribute to our Health of body as Tranquillity of Soul.

Sir George Etheredge

Letter to the Duke of Buckingham,
12 November 1688

DRINKING

The thirsty earth soaks up the rain,
And drinks, and gapes for drink again.
The plants suck in the earth, and are
With constant drinking fresh and fair;
The sea itself — which one would think
Should have but little need of drink -
Drinks ten thousand rivers up,
So filled that they o'er flow the cup.
The busy sun — and one would guess
By's drunken fiery face no less —
Drinks up the sea, and when he's done,
The moon and stars drink up the sun:
They drink and dance by their own light,
They drink and revel all the night.
Nothing in Nature's sober found,
But an eternal health goes round.
Fill up the bowl, then, fill it high,
Fill up the glasses there; for why
Should ever creature drink but I:
Why, man of morals, tell me why?

ABRAHAM COWLEY

MAN IS AN EPICURE

I became aware that I was eating something particularly delicious, soft-boiled eggs embedded in a layer of meat jelly, seasoned with herbs, and discreetly iced. To please Marambot I smacked my lips.

'First-rate, this.'

He smiled.

'The two essential ingredients are good jelly, which is not easily procured, and good eggs. How rare they are, really good eggs, with reddish yolks, and the proper flavour. I keep two poultry yards, one for eggs and one for the fowls for the table. I have a special method of feeding my layers. I have my own ideas on the subject. In an egg, just as in chicken, beef, mutton or milk, you recover, and you should be able to taste, the extract, the quintessence of all the food that the animal has consumed. How much better people would fare if they paid more attention to that point.'

'I see you are an epicure,' I laughed.

'I should think so. So is everyone who isn't an idiot. Man is an epicure just as he is an artist, a scholar, a poet. The palate, my dear fellow, is as delicate and susceptible of training as the eye or ear, and equally deserving of respect. To be without a sense of taste is to be deficient in an exquisite faculty, that of appreciating the quality of comestibles, just as a person may lack the faculty of appreciating the quality of a book or a work of art. It is to want a vital sense, one of the elements of human superiority.

'It consigns a man to one of the innumerable categories of cripples, degenerates and fools, of which our race is composed. In a word, it implies an alimentary stupidity, precisely on a footing with mental deficiency. A man who cannot tell a crayfish from a lobster, or a herring, that admirable fish which comprises all the different flavours and essences of the sea, from a mackerel or a whiting, or a William pear from a Duchess, may be compared to a man who cannot distinguish Balzac from Eugène Sue, a Beethoven symphony from a military march by a regimental bandmaster, the Apollo Belvedere from the statue of Général de Blanmont.'

GUY DE MAUPASSANT
Madame Husson's Rose-king

SPECTATOR AB EXTRA

As I sat at the Café I said to myself,
They may talk as they please about what they call pelf,
They may sneer as they like about eating and drinking,
But help it I cannot, I cannot help thinking
  How pleasant it is to have money, heigh-ho!
  How pleasant it is to have money.

I sit at my table *en grande seigneur*,
And when I have done, throw a crust to the poor;
Not only the pleasure itself of good living,
But also the pleasure of now and then giving:
  So pleasant it is to have money, heigh-ho!
  So pleasant it is to have money.

They talk as they please about what they call pelf,
And how one ought never to think of one's self,
How pleasures of thought surpass eating and drinking—
My pleasure of thought is the pleasure of thinking
  How pleasant it is to have money, heigh-ho!
  How pleasant it is to have money.

Glassware, from *Mrs Beeton's Book of Household Management*, 1849

TABLE GLASS.

2 Decanters.— 2 Claret Jugs.— Caraffe.— Water Jug and Glass.— 9 Wine Glasses.— 3 Champagne Tumblers.— 1 Soda Glass.— 3 Tumblers.— 2 Glass Dishes.— 1 Cream Ewer and Sugar Bowl.— 2 Ice Plates.— 2 Finger Basins.— 1 Glass Centre Piece.—

Roast Fowl.

Pheasant.

Game Pie with Jelly.

Shrimp Patties.

Oyster Patties.

Lobster Salad.

Savoury Jelly a la Bellevue.

Brawn.

Pigeon Pie

Galantine of Veal.

Russian Salad.

Crayfish.

Ham Garnished.

Tongue Garnished.

SUPPER DISHES.

Le Dîner

Come along, 'tis the time, ten or more minutes past,
And he who came first had to wait for the last;
The oysters ere this had been in and been out;
Whilst I have been sitting and thinking about
    How pleasant it is to have money, heigh-ho!
    How pleasant it is to have money.

A clear soup with eggs; *voilà tout*; of the fish
The *filets de sole* are a moderate dish
A la Orly, but you're for red mullet, you say:
By the gods of good fare, who can question to-day
    How pleasant it is to have money, heigh-ho!
    How pleasant it is to have money.

After oysters, sauterne; then sherry, Champagne,
Ere one bottle goes, comes another again;
Fly up, thou bold cork, to the ceiling above,
And tell to our ears in the sound that they love
    How pleasant it is to have money, heigh-ho!
    How pleasant it is to have money.

Supper dishes, from *Mrs Beeton's Book of Household Management*, 1849

I've the simplest of palates; absurd it may be,
But I almost could dine on a *poulet-au-riz,*
Fish and soup and omelette and that — but the deuce -
There were to be woodcocks, and not Charlotte Russe!
　So pleasant it is to have money, heigh-ho!
　So pleasant it is to have money.

Your Chablis is acid, away with the Hock,
Give me the pure juice of the purple Médoc:
St Peray is exquisite; but if you please,
Some Burgundy just before tasting the cheese.
　So pleasant it is to have money, heigh-ho!
　So pleasant it is to have money.

As for that, pass the bottle, and d — n the expense,
I've seen it observed by a writer of sense,
That the labouring classes could scarce live a day,
If people like us didn't eat, drink, and pay.
　So useful it is to have money, heigh-ho!
　So useful it is to have money.

One ought to be grateful, I quite apprehend,
Having dinner and supper and plenty to spend,
And so suppose now, while the things go away,
By way of a grace we all stand up and say:
  How pleasant it is to have money, heigh-ho!
  How pleasant it is to have money.

ARTHUR HUGH CLOUGH

THE FIVE REASONS

If all be true that I do think,
There are *Five Reasons* we should drink;
Good Wine, a Friend, or being Dry,
Or lest we should be by and by;
Or any other Reason why.

DEAN HENRY ALDRICH

BALLADE OF SOPORIFIC ABSORPTION

Ho! Ho! Yes! Yes! It's very all well,
You may drunk I am think, but I'll tell you I'm not,
I'm as sound as a fiddle and as fit as a bell,
And stable quite ill to see what's what.
I under *do* stand you surprise a got
When I headed my smear with gooseberry jam:
And I've swallowed, I grant, a beer of a lot -
But I'm not so think as you drunk I am.

Can I liquor my stand? Why, yes, like hell!
I care not how many a tossed I've pot,
I shall stralk quite weight and not yutter an ell,
My feet will not spalter the least little jot:
If you knownly had own! — well I have him a dot,
And I said to him 'Sergeant, I'll come like a lamb -
The floor it seems like a storm in a yacht,
But I'm not so think as you drunk I am.'

For example to prove it I'll tale you a tell -
I once knew a fellow named Apricot —
I'm sorry, I just chair over a fell —

A trifle — this chap, on a very day hot -
If I hadn't consumed that last whisky of tot! —
As I said now, this fellow called Abraham -
Ah? One more? Since it's you! Just a do me will spot -
But I'm not so think as you drunk I am.

Envoi

So, Prince, you suggest I bolted my shot?
Well, like what you say, and soul your damn!
I'm an upple litset by the talk you rot -
But I'm not so think as you drunk I am.

Sir J. C. Squire

Athol Brose

Charm'd with a drink which Highlanders compose,
A German traveller exclaim'd with glee, -
Potztausend! Sare, if dis is Athol Brose,
How goot dere Athol Boetry must be!

Thomas Hood

Moderation in All Things

We now have made in one design
The Utile and Dulce join,
And taught the poor and men of wealth
To reconcile their tastes to health.
Restrain each forward appetite
To dine with prudence and delight,
And, careful all our rules to follow,
To masticate before they swallow.
'Tis thus Hygeia guides our pen
To warn the greedy sons of men
To moderate their wine and meat
And eat to live, not live to eat.

Dr William Kitchiner
Apicius Redivivus, or The Cook's Oracle (1817)

To Youth

Drink wine, and live here blithefull, while ye may:
The morrowes life too late is, live to-day.

Robert Herrick

TRIALS OF A DYSPEPTIC

'Lunch, sir? Yes-ser, pickled salmon,
Cutlets, Kidneys, Greens, and – Gammon!'
Have you got no wholesome meat, sir?
Flesh or fowl that one can eat, sir?'
'Eat, sir? Yes-ser, on the dresser.
Pork, sir?' Pork, sir, I detest, sir -
'Lobsters?' Are to me unblest, sir -
'Duck and peas?' I can't digest, sir –
'Puff, sir?' Stuff sir! 'Fish, sir?' Pish, sir!
'Sausage?' Sooner eat the dish, sir -
'Shrimps, sir? Prawns, sir? Crawfish? Winkle?
Scallops ready in a twinkle?
Wilks and cockles, crabs to follow!'
Heav'ns, *nothing* I can swallow!
WAITER!
'YES-SAR.'
Bread for twenty -
I shall starve in midst of plenty!

H. CHOLMONDELEY-PENNELL

Cooks and Cookery

A cook may be taught, but a man who
can roast is born with the faculty.

Brillat-Savarin

THE DUTIES OF THE COOK

The cook however, is at the head of the kitchen; and in proportion to her possession of the qualities of cleanliness, neatness, order, regularity, and celerity of action, so will her influence appear in the conduct of those who are under her; as it is upon her that the whole responsibility of the business of the kitchen rests, whilst the others must lend her both a ready and a willing assistance, and be especially tidy in their appearance, and active in their movements.

Early rising
In a cook, this quality is most essential, for an hour lost in the morning will keep her toiling, absolutely toiling, all day, to overtake that which might otherwise been achieved with ease.

MRS ISABELLA BEETON
The Book of Household Management, Entirely New Edition, 1899

ADVICE TO COOKS

Most knowing Sir! the greatest part of Cooks
Searching for truth, and couzan'd by its Looks,
One wou'd have all things little, hence has try'd
Turkey Poults fresh from th' Egg in Batter fry'd
Others, to shew the largeness of their Soul,
Prepare you Muttons swol'd and Oxen whole.
To vary the same things some think is Art.
By larding of Hogs-feet and Bacon Tart.
The Tast is now to that Perfection brought
That care, when wanting Skill, creates the Fault.
Be cautious how you change old Bills of Fare,
Such alterations shou'd at least be rare;
Yet credit to the Artist will acrue,
Who in known things still makes th' appearance new,
Fresh Dainties are by Britain's Traffik known,
And now by constant Use familiar grown;
What Lord of old wou'd bid his Cook prepare
Mangoes, Botargo, Champignons, Caviare?
Or wou'd our thrum-cap'd Ancestors find fault
For want of Sugar-Tongs or Spoons for Salt.

DR WILLIAM KING
The Art of Cookery (1709)

The illustrated frontispiece of *The Queen's Royal Cookery or, Expert and Ready Way for the Dressing of all Sorts of Flesh, Fowl, Fish ... With the Art of Preserving and Candying of Fruits and Flowers.* By T Hall, London,

THE
QUEEN'S Royal
COOKERY:
OR,

Expert and ready Way for the Dressing of all Sorts of Flesh, Fowl, Fish : Either Baked, Boiled, Roasted, Stewed, Fryed, Boiled, Hashed, Frigasied, Carbonaded, Forced, Collared, Soused, Dried, &c. After the Best and Newest Way, With their several Sauces and Sallads.

And making all Sorts of PICKLES.

ALSO

Making Variety of Pies, Pasties, Tarts, Cheese-Cakes, Custards, Creams, &c.

WITH

The ART of Preserving and Candying of Fruits and Flowers ; and the making of Conserves, Syrups, Jellies, and Cordial Waters, Also making several Sorts of English Wines, Cyder, Mead, Metheglin.

TOGETHER

With several Cosmetick or Beautifying Waters · And also several Sorts of Essences and Sweet Waters : By Persons of the Highest Quality.

By T. Hall, *Free Cook of* London.

The Fourth Edition.

London: Printed for S. Bates, at the Sun and Bible in Gilt-spur-street, in Pye-corner: And A. Bettesworth, at the Red Lyon in Pater-noster row. 1729.

Licensed according to Order.

1729, bearing the portrait of Queen Anne; preparation of food in a kitchen and two smaller illustrations with the titles 'Pastry' and 'Chymistry'

ESCAPE ROUTE

I have never been able to find in writing the escape from external things that I find in cooking. Cooking takes my mind off everything but itself, for the reason that I am not a seasoned cook and therefore have to think and concentrate. At the same time this concentration is effortless – unlike the concentration involved in literary work, which is so very effortful that if there be any real opposition from outside I can make no headway against it. There is, too, in writing an emotional drain which can eventually bring about complete exhaustion; but in cooking, fatigue is bodily and passes away with rest.

SHEILA KAYE-SMITH
Kitchen Fugue

PHILOSOPHICAL PRINCIPLES

The subject of cookery having been very naturally introduced at a table where Johnson, who boasted of the niceness of his palate, avowed that 'he always found a good dinner'. He said, 'I could write a better book about cookery than has ever been written; it should be a book upon philosophical principles. Pharmacy is now made much more simple. Cookery may be so, too. A prescription, which is now compounded of five ingredients, had formerly fifty in it. So in Cookery. If the nature of the ingredients is well-known, much fewer will do. Then, as you cannot make bad meat good, I would tell you what is the best butcher's meat, the best beef, the best pieces; how to choose young fowls; the proper seasons of different vegetables; and how to roast, and boil, and compound.'

JAMES BOSWELL
The Life of Samuel Johnson

THE MEANING OF COOKERY

What does cookery mean? It means the knowledge of Medea and of Circe, and of Calypso, and Sheba.

It means knowledge of all herbs, and fruits, and balms and spices, and of all that is healing and sweet in grapes and savoury in meat.

It means carefulness, and inventiveness, watchfulness, willingness, and readiness of appliance.

It means the economy of your great-grandmother and the science of modern chemistry, and French art, and Arabian hospitality.

It means, in fine, that you are to see imperatively that everyone has something nice to eat.

JOHN RUSKIN

An English family at table under a *punkah* or fan kept in motion by a *khelassy*. From *The Costume and Customs of Modern India*, by Captain Thomas Williamson, illustrated by Sir Charles D'Oyly, London, c. 1824

VIII.

London, Published & Sold by Edwd. Orme, March 1st 1813.

An English Family at Table, under a Punkah, or Fan,
kept in motion by a Khelasy.

MY CHINEE COOK

They who say the bush is dull are not
so very far astray,
For this Eucalyptic cloisterdom
is anything but gay;
But its uneventful dulness,
I contentedly could brook,
If I could only get back my lost,
lamented Chinee cook.

We had tried them without number,
cooks to wit — my wife and I —
One a week, then three a fortnight,
as my wife can testify;
But at last we got the right one;
I may say 'twas by a fluke,
For he dropped in miscellaneous-like,
that handy Chinee cook.

He found the kitchen empty,
laid his swag down and commenced;

The Viceroy of Canton, sitting at table with Lord Macartney
in the hall of the East India Company's factory, December
1793, during Lord Macartney's embassy to China. From
Drawings of William and Samuel Daniell, China, 1793

My wife, surprised, found nothing
to say anything against;
But she asked him for how much a year
the work he undertook,
'Me workee for me ration,'
said that noble Chinee cook...

We got fat upon his cooking,
we were happy in those days,
For he tickled up our palates
in a thousand pleasant ways.
Oh, his dinners! Oh, his dinners!
They were fit for any duke!
Oh, delectable Mongolian!
Oh, celestial Chinee cook!

... And day by day upon my wife
and me the mystery grew,
How his virtues were so many and
his earnings were so few;
And we laid our heads together
to find by hook or crook,
The secret of the cheapness of
that priceless Chinee cook...

But one day when I was out
he brought my wife a lot of things,
Turquoise earrings, opal bracelets,
ruby brooches, diamond rings,
And he ran their various prices
o'er as glibly as a book,
And dirt cheap were the jewels
of that jewel of a cook.

I returned, and just in time
to stop the purchase of the lot.
And to ask him where on earth
these costly jewels he had got.
And when I looked him in the face,
good gracious, how he shook!
And he says, says he 'Me bought him,'
did that trembling Chinee cook.

And I a justice of the peace!
Oh, fortune, how unkind!
For a certain Sidney robbery
came rushing to my mind.
'You bought them! Ah, I fear me, John,
you paid them with a hook;

I am bound to apprehend you,
oh, unhappy Chinee cook!'

So the mystery was solved at length,
the secret now we saw:
John used us as a refuge
from the clutches of the law;
And now, alas, too late,
would I his frailty overlook,
He's gone and I am left without
my skilful Chinee cook...

Take away the hateful letters.
'Twas my justice robbed my peace.
Take my name from the commission,
and my matchless cook release.
But I fear my Johnnie's dead,
for I am haunted by a spook,
With oblique eyes and a pig-tail,
like my lost, my Chinee cook.

J. B. Stephens

A cook thei hadde with them for the nonce,
To boyle chikens and the marrow bones,
And to make powders swete and testen wel.
Wel coude he knowe a draught of London ale.
He coude roste, sethe, broille, and frie,
Make soupe and brawn and bake wel a pye.
But gret harm was it, as it seemed me,
That on his shin a sore wound had he;
For blankemange he made with the beste.

GEOFFREY CHAUCER
Canterbury Tales

Rôti sans Pareil

Take a large olive, stone it and stuff it with a paste made of anchovy, capers and oil.

Put the olive inside a trussed and boned bec-figue (garden warbler).

Put the bec-fugue inside a fat ortolan.

Put the ortolan inside a boned lark.

Put the stuffed lark inside a boned thrush.

Put the thrush inside a fat quail.

Put the quail, wrapped in vine-leaves, inside a boned lapwing.

Put the lapwing inside a boned golden plover.

Put the plover inside a fat, boned, red-legged partridge.

Put the partridge inside a young, boned, and well-hung woodcock.

Put the woodcock, rolled in bread-crumbs, inside a boned teal.

Put the teal inside a boned guinea-fowl.

Put the guinea-fowl, well-larded, inside a young and boned tame duck.

Put the duck inside a boned and fat fowl.

Put the fowl inside a well-hung pheasant.

Put the pheasant inside a boned and fat wild goose.

Put the goose inside a fine turkey.

Put the turkey inside a boned bustard.

Having arranged your roast after this fashion, place it in a saucepan of proper size with onions stuffed with cloves, carrots, small squares of ham, celery, mignonette, several strips of bacon well-seasoned, pepper, salt, spice, coriander seeds, and two cloves of garlic.

Seal the saucepan hermetically by closing it with pastry. Then put it for ten hours over a gentle fire and arrange it so that the heat penetrates evenly. An oven moderately heated would suit better than the hearth.

Before serving, remove the pastry, put your roast on a hot dish after removing the grease, if there is any, and serve.

Venus in the Kitchen or Love's Cookery Book
Edited by Norman Douglas

Scripture Cake

1. 4 ½ cups of Kings iv. 22 v.
2. 1 ½ cups of Judges v. 25 v.
3. 2 cups of Jeremiah vi. 20 v.
4. 2 cups of I Samuel xxv. 18 v.
5. 2 cups of Nahum iii. 12 v.
6. 1 cup of Numbers xvii. 8 v.
7. 2 tablespoonsful I Sam. xiv. 25 v.
8. Season to taste II Chron. ix. 9 v.
9. 6 cups Jeremiah xvii. II v.
10. 1 pinch Leviticus ii. 13 v.
11. 1 cup of Judges iv. 19 last clause.
12. 3 teaspoonsful Amos iv. 5 v.
13. Follow Solomon's prescription for the making of a good boy and you will have a good cake, see Proverbs xxiii. 14 v.

AMY ATKINSON AND GRACE HOLROYD
Practical Cookery

Breakfast and tea china, from *Mrs Beeton's Book of Household Management*, 1849

BREAKFAST AND TEA CHINA.

4 Tea Cups ... 2 Bread and Butter Plates ... 1 Teapot ... 1 Butter Dish ... 1 Sardine Box ... 2 Coffee Cups ...
Afternoon Tea Set ... 1 Milk Jug ... 1 Jug ... 1 Bread Dish ... 1 Bacon Dish ... 1 Marmalade Jar ... 4 Breakfast Cups ...

Woman sweetmeat-seller. Inscribed: 'Cake-seller', 1830–40

'Grain-seller', gouache on mica, 1830–40.

SOUPS.

1—Mutton Broth. 2—Pot-au-Feu. 3—Tomato Soup. 4—Kidney Soup.
5—Consommé à la Celestine. 6—Consommé à la Royale. 7—Bonne Femme.
8—Hollandaise. 9—Consommé à la Julienne. 10—Consommé à la Brunoise.

Frogs' Legs

Put three dozen frogs' legs in a saucepan with a dozen chopped mushrooms, four shallots also chopped, and two ounces of butter. Toss them on a fire for five minutes; then add a tablespoon of flour, a little salt and pepper, grated nutmeg; and moisten with a glass of white wine and a teacupful of consommé.

Boil for ten minutes. Meanwhile mix the yolks of four eggs with two tablespoons of cream. Now remove the frogs' legs and the other ingredients from the fire, then add the eggs and cream, stirring continually until thoroughly mixed, and serve.

A noble aphrodisiac.

Venus in the Kitchen or Love's Cookery Book
Edited by Norman Douglas

Soup dishes, from *Mrs Beeton's Book of Household Management*, 1849

CHRISTMAS FARE

At Christmas time be careful of your fame;
See the old tenant's table be the same.
Then if you would send up the brawner's head,
Sweet rosemary and bays around it spread;
His foaming tusks let some large pippin grace,
Or mid'st those thund'ring spears an orange place,
Sauce like himself, offensive to its foes,
The roguish mustard, dang'rous to the nose,
Sack and the well-spiced Hippocras the wine.
Wassail the bowl with ancient ribbands fine,
Porridge with plumbs, and turkeys with the chine.

DR WILLIAM KING
The Art of Cookery (1709)

BAROMETER SOUP

I hunted up another barometer; it was new and perfect. I boiled it half an hour in a pot of bean soup which the cooks were making. The result was unexpected: the instrument was not affected at all but there was such a strong barometer taste to the soup that the head cook, who was a most conscientious person, changed its name in the bill of fare. The dish was so liked by all that I ordered the cook to have barometer soup every day.

MARK TWAIN
A Tramp Abroad

The discovery of a new dish confers more happiness on humanity than the discovery of a new star.

BRILLAT-SAVARIN

EATING IN
FOREIGN PARTS

Nothing helps scenery like ham and eggs.

MARK TWAIN

Innocents Abroad

We are getting foreignized rapidly, and with facility. We are getting reconciled to halls and bed-chambers with unhomelike stone floors, and no carpets: floors that ring to the tread of one's heels with a sharpness that is death to sentimental musing. We are getting used to tidy, noiseless waiters, who glide hither and thither, and hover about your back and your elbows like butterflies, quick to comprehend orders, quick to fill them; thankful for a gratuity without regard to the amount; and always polite — never otherwise than polite. That is the strangest curiosity yet: a really polite hotel waiter who isn't an idiot...

We are getting used to ice frozen by artificial process in ordinary bottles — the only kind of ice they have here. We are getting used to all these things; but we are not getting used to carrying our own soap. We are sufficiently civilized to carry our own combs and tooth-brushes; but this thing of having to ring for soap every time we wash is new to us, and not pleasant at all. We think of it just after we get our heads and faces thoroughly wet, or just when we think we have been in the bath-tub long enough, and then, of course, an annoying delay follows. These Marseillaises make Marsellaise hymns, and Marseilles vests, and Marseilles soap for all the world; but they never sing their hymns, or wear their vests, or wash with their soap themselves.

We have learned to go through the lingering routine of the *table d'hôte* with patience, with serenity, with satisfaction. We take soup; then wait a few minutes for the fish; a few minutes more and the plates are changed, and the roast beef comes; another change and we take peas; change again and take lentils; change and take snail patties (I prefer grasshoppers); change and take roast chicken and salad; then strawberry pie and ice cream; then green figs, pears, oranges, green almonds, etc; finally coffee. Wine with every course, of course, being in France. With such a cargo on board, digestion is a slow process, and we must sit long in the cool chambers and smoke and read French newspapers, which have a strange fashion of telling a perfectly straight story till you get to the 'nub' of it, and then a word drops in that no man can translate, and that story is ruined. An embankment fell on some Frenchman yesterday, and the papers are full of it to-day, but whether those sufferers were killed, or crippled, or bruised, or only scared, is more than I can possibly make out, and yet I would just give anything to know.

We were troubled a little at dinner to-day, by the conduct of an American, who talked very loudly and coarsely, and laughed boisterously where all others were so quiet and well-behaved. He ordered wine with a royal flourish, and said: 'I never dine without wine, sir,' (which was a pitiful falsehood), and looked around upon the company to bask in the admiration he expected to find in their faces. All these airs in a land where they would as soon expect to leave the soup out of the bill of fare as the wine! — in a land where wine is nearly as common among all ranks as water! This fellow said: 'I am a free-born sovereign, sir, an American, sir, and I want everybody to know it!'

He did not mention that he was a lineal descendant of Balaam's ass, but everybody knew that without his telling it.

MARK TWAIN
The Innocents Abroad

'Our Burra Khana': Europeans feast in the street, surrounded by Indian servants. From *Curry & Rice* by George Franklin (1822-59)

OUR BURRA KHANA

DESSERT.

THE GOOD FOOD GUIDE

'If you lose your way and cannot tell what to eat,' said the Choco Indian Ailipio, 'then you must look for a tree where monkeys are sitting. You will find it most easily by making for the noise. Monkeys are extremely wasteful in their eating. Usually they take only one bite of a fruit, and then drop it to pick another which has caught their eye. For every one they eat, often they take four or five merely to play with and throw away again. These fruits or nuts can be picked up without fear, for you may be sure what the monkeys like, we can eat, too.'

PER HØST
What the World Showed Me

The destiny of nations depends on the manner in which they are fed.

BRILLAT-SAVARIN

Dessert dishes, from *Mrs Beeton's Book of Household Management*, 1849

A Surfeit of Turtle

We lived at Ega, during most part of the year, on turtle. The great fresh-water turtle of the Amazons grows on the upper river to an immense size, a full-grown one measuring nearly three feet in length by two in breadth, and is a load for the strongest Indian. Every house has a little pond called a *curral* (pen), in the back-yard to hold a stock of the animals through the season of dearth — the wet months; those who have a number of Indians in their employ sending them out for a month when the waters are low, to collect a stock, and those who have not, purchasing their supply; with some difficulty, however, as they are rarely offered for sale. The price of turtles, like that of all other articles of food, has risen greatly with the introduction of steam-vessels... The flesh is very tender, palatable and wholesome; but it is very cloying; every one ends, sooner or later, by becoming thoroughly surfeited. I became so sick of turtle in the course of two years that I could not bear the smell of it, although at the same time nothing else was to be had, and I was suffering actual hunger. The native women cook it in various ways. The entrails are chopped up and made into a delicious soup called *sarapatel*, which is generally boiled in the concave upper shell of the animal used as a kettle. The tender flesh of the breast is partially minced with farinha, and the breast shell then roasted over the fire, making a very pleasant dish. Steaks cut from the breast and cooked with the fat form another palatable dish. Large sausages are made of the thick-coated stomach, which is filled with minced meat and boiled. The quarters cooked in a kettle of Tucupi sauce form another variety of food. When surfeited with turtle in all other shapes, pieces of the lean part roasted on a spit and moistened only with vinegar make an agreeable change. The smaller kind of turtle, the *tracaja*, which makes its appearance in the main river, and lays its eggs a month earlier than the large species, is of less utility to the inhabitants although its flesh is superior, on account of the difficulty of keeping it alive; it survives captivity but a very few days...

HENRY WALTER BATES
The Naturalist on the Amazons (1863)

CHOPSTICKS AND ALL

We dined one night with Mr Kao, the Chinese Consul-General, another English couple name of Scott (M.O.I.), another Chinaman, Martin, Tony and I. The meal was a *chinoiserie*, chopsticks and all. The house was a European disgrace, full of photographs of Chiang Kai-Shek and scrolls of characters, treated as Titians, not texts.

'Whose calligraphy is that, Mr Kao?' I gathered from Tony was the correct question. There was a grog-tray on the terrace, bearing a hundred bottles, many of which are only seen in bars, like Crème de Cacao, de Viollette and Crème besides every known spirit and aperitif. After some adventurous drinks we sat down to a table of Mr Kao's own design. It was round, and the centre of its circle (in diameter about a yard) whizzed round dumb-waiter fashion — very ingenious and well-suited to Bognor. Soup first, next a very small spatchcocked sucking-pig with sly unspatched, almost-human face and the crackliest of skins, eaten from the centre dish with chopsticks.

The host, Mr Kao, handled an extra pair of sticks for passing delicacies to his guests. Then a fish *à la nage* in its own *bouillon*, thin shark's fins swimming in the same, followed by cabbage and mushrooms sweetly blended. Then — East compromising with West — a chicken pie very unlike ours. A delicious dish of sweet-sour something came next, and then little bags of suet containing I don't really know what — a great many eaten by each guest (Duff made a beast of himself) and we *wound up* with a nice delicate duck soup. All very good, eaten out of little Chinese bowls with sticks and all tasting, to my amateur palate, identical.

Conversation was restricted to food-subjects with occasional health-drinking. If Tony said, 'You're a wonderful man, Mr Kao' in a rollicking way, Mr Kao would grin and say, 'You think so, Mr Keswick? You think so?' delighted and in part believing it. Mrs Kao, a dear woman, was the fifteen-stone skeleton of the feast, having no English. She all but wept in the ladies' lu when she explained to me in pidgin how fond she was of conversation...

DIANA COOPER
Trumpets from the Steep

Forks and Their Uses

I observed a custome in all those Italian cities and townes through which I passed, that is not used in any other country that I saw in my travels, neither doe I thinke that any other nation of Christendome doth use in but only Italy. The Italian, and also most strangers that are commorant, in Italy, doe alwaies at their meals use a little forke, when they cut their meate. For while with their knife which they hold in one hande they cut the meat out of the dish, they fasten their forke, which they hold in their other hande, upon the same dish, so that whatsoever he be that sitting in the company of any others at meale, should unadvisedly touch the dish of meate with his fingers, from which all at the table do cut, he will give occasion of offence unto the company, as having transgressed the laws of good manners, insomuch that for his error he shall be at the least browbeaten, if not reprehended in wordes.

This forme of feeding I understand is generally used in all places of Italy, their forkes being for the most part made of yron or steele, and some of silver, but those are used only by gentlemen. The reason of this their curiosity is, because the Italian cannot be any means indure to have his dish touched with fingers, seeing all men's fingers are not alike cleane.

THOMAS CORYATE
Coryate's Crudities hastily gobbled up in Five Month's Travel (1611)

EPIGRAM ON AN ACADEMIC VISIT TO THE CONTINENT

I went to Frankfort, and got drunk
With that most learn'd professor Brunck:
I went to Worts, and got more drunken
With that more learn'd professor Ruhncken.

RICHARD PORSON

PERUVIAN MEALS

Every few days our friend Señor Gomez from the steamship office would lay in our hands a sheaf of pink meal tickets. These stated that the bearer, 'Grace Tourist', was good for a meal at any one of the various hostelries. Now at our hotel there was a vast *table d'hôte* dining room on the main floor which was cold, pale, and tardy of service; the food was (if I may be frank) uninspired except the ever-delicious *palta*, a kind of alligator pear, and the glorious coffee.

The roast beef and cabinet pudding and that sort of thing were rather dreary after our exciting meals aboard ship. I believe some sort of waiters' strike was in progress, which may have embarrassed the management; at any rate, our attempts to elicit something as apparently simple as orange juice (*jugo de naranjas*, if you can manage those 'js') would have caused laughter in a dinosaur. But downstairs in the basement was a little grillroom, with bright lights, and dancing, and meats turning warmly on a spit. Many times did the waiter explain to us that the pink

Oranges

Apples

Pears

tickets were no good in the grill, only upstairs. We firmly refused to understand. We gradually made the round of the grill's excellent menu, particularly *corbina* (a delicious fish), *lomo de chancho* (loin of pork), *rinones de cordero* (lamb's kidneys) and *cabrito* (little goat), laid a generous tip beside the pink tickets, murmured the prayer-book rubric 'collect for Grace', and left the *mozo* to argue it out with the *maître d'hotel*.

The pleasures of dealing with an unknown language are impossible to exaggerate. I think the children's favourite word on the menu was *panqueque*, which was not hard to guess among the *postres* (excellent term for dessert). But they were disappointed when they ordered *ciruelas*, which sound so exotic, and found them the homely prune.

CHRISTOPHER MORELY
Hasta la Vista

Monkey Business

The Rest House was perched on the edge of the precipice with a view of the gorge and was available for picnics and most popular, being only a dozen miles from Jubbulpore, where my battalion was then stationed. On the occasion I refer to, I and two companions had arranged a party of six on a hot weather night *au clair de lune*, and had taken out with us a sumptuous meal. This was laid on a table just outside the bungalow some ten yards from the veranda, where the party of six was sitting. The servants were just announcing that everything was ready when there was a terrible commotion — a mob of fifty or sixty langoors, the big grey and black Indian monkey — came leaping up from the rocks, overran the plateau, upset the table, scattered the glasses and bottles and cutlery, and disappeared as quickly as they had come with every morsel of our beautiful dinner. All that remained was to drive home twelve miles and scratch up some beer and sandwiches.

Sir Francis Colchester-Wemyss
Wine and Food, 29

Diplomat's Disappointment

I am disappointed not to find upon this boat the variety of puddings to which I had looked forward. One of the to me more distressing manifestations of the changing world in which I live, is that the fashion for puddings had almost wholly faded. As a child, when staying at Clandeboye or Shanganagh, there were always two different puddings at every meal. We were offered College Pudding, Bachelor's Pudding, Hasty Pudding, Tipsy Pudding, Treacle Pudding, Lemon Sponge, Pancakes, Junket, Coconut Custard, Marmalade Pie, Roly Poly, Suet Pudding, Toffee Pudding, Almond Sponge, Cherry Whirl, Coffee Honeycomb, Apple Charlotte, Macaroon Hasties, Meringues, Marshmallows, Smyrna Mould, and all manner of tarts and creams.

Moreover, before the first war, a 'luncheon cake' was always handed round with the cheese. V. does not herself care for sweet dishes and prefers those sour concoctions which are called 'savouries' although they so seldom are. In fact I feel that she regards my passion for puddings as effeminate or perhaps Scottish, or perhaps middle-class. Although at Sissinghurst I am pampered with the best tarts that I have ever known, I am not offered these delicacies at my club. Day after day, luncheon after luncheon, dinner after dinner, does the menu bear the single word 'semolina', and although ices are also provided I happen to hate ice. When once I dared to suggest to our secretary (who although a generous man does not enjoy pandering to any form of decadence), that I might have a soufflé for dinner, his face fell abruptly and in contempt. 'But that,' he said sharply, 'would mean getting in another chef.' I did not have the courage to pursue the theme.

I had hoped none the less that the *Willem Ruys*, with her long Teutonic tradition of puddings, and considering the lavish variety of fish, meat and game that she provides, would at last give me the pudding opportunity that I have, since the age of fourteen, been denied. I was thus delighted when I saw on the menu such suggestive varieties as 'Malakoff Pudding', 'Rubane Pudding', 'Harlekin Pudding' and 'Noga Ijs'. But when I called for these delicacies night after night, I discovered that they were in fact what in British restaurant-cars are called 'shape', being little dabs the size and form of a child's sand-pie and differing from each other solely owing to the fact that some contained specks of angelica and some bits of orange or ginger. I must therefore resign myself in future to the fact that the puddings of my childhood have, even as fourwheelers, passed from circulation.

SIR HAROLD NICOLSON
Journey to Java

There was an Old Man of the East,
Who gave all his children a feast;
But they all ate so much,
And their conduct was such,
That it killed that Old Man of the East

EDWARD LEAR

Sardines in Sand

By this time we felt that our own little effort to draw a new red line across a survey map was very small and insignificant and that we should certainly be able to walk to Jaghabub carrying a fanatis and a tin of corned beef if necessary! We were much less confident of it next morning, however, when all the camels turned up their noses at the date food offered them and deliberately ran away.

There was nowhere for them to run to among the dunes, so we got them back after a laborious half hour, but felt that the word *agal* and not Kufara would be written across my heart in future! There was no fire that morning, and uncooked soaked rice is not appetizing. I remember I was tying the remains of my stocking round my feet when I heard a gloomy voice say: 'We ate the last box of sardines last night because you lost the beef-tin-opener in the sand and the rice is coal black. I wish you would not be so miserly with the fanatis water!'

I didn't pay much attention as I hadn't any more stockings. Evidently the primrose and scarlet boots which I had bought for four *mejidies* (sixteen shillings) at Jof were not suited for walking, for I had been wearing two pairs of woollen stockings one over the other and now they all hung in shreds round my feet.

However, I did look up when the plaintive tones continued. 'I've found one sardine. He must have fallen out when you upset the canteen in the sand.' With horror I saw a soddened, dark mass and on the top of it a minute yellow block shaped like a fish, but I did not like to be discouraging.

'Are you sure that there is a sardine inside that sand?' I asked diffidently.

Hassanein was offended. 'Will you carve him or shall I?' he asked majestically.

ROSITA FORBES
The Secret of the Sahara: Kufara

Headaches and Vapours

At two o'clock we sat down to table *en famille*. I was placed between the Marchioness and her husband. The dinner was served in plate, and the huge massy dishes brought up by a vast train of gentlemen and chaplains, several of them decorated with the Order of Christ. This attendance had quite a feudal air…

The Portuguese had need have the stomach of ostriches to digest the loads of greasy victuals with which they cram themselves. Their vegetables, their rice, their poultry are all stewed in the essence of ham, and so strongly seasoned with pepper and spices that a spoonful of pease or a quarter of an onion is sufficient to set one's mouth in a flame. With such a diet and the continual swallowing of sweetmeats, I am not surprised at their complaining continually of headaches and vapours. The rain descending with violence, every window was shut, and the absence of vegetable perfumes from the garden, so delightful after a shower, supplied by a steam of burnt lavender.

The Journal of William Beckford in Portugal and Spain, 1787–8

Invalid trays, from *Mrs Beeton's Book of Household Management, 1849*

1—Steamed Fillets of Sole, Fairy Toast, Beef Tea, Baked Custard, Barley Water.
2—Toast, Fried Soles and Potato Straws, Beef Tea, Lemonade, Jelly.
3—Clear Soup, Lamb Cutlet. Mashed Potato and Spinach, Milanaise Soufflé,
Lemonade, Tomato Sauce.

A Cut off the Joint

They were up long before us, and had breakfast on raw meat cut from a large joint which lay, without regard to cleanliness, among the deposits on the floor of the igloo. Their mode of eating was ingeniously active. They cut the meat in long strips, introduced one end into the mouth, swallowed it as far as the powers of deglutition would allow, and then, cutting off the protruding portion close to the lips, prepared themselves for a second mouthful. It was really a feat of address: those of us who tried it failed awkwardly; and yet I have seen infants in the mother's hood, not two years old, who managed to perform it without accident.

ELISHA KENT KANE
Arctic Exploration in Search of Sir John Franklin (1898)

'Badhak or Qassab, The Caste of Butcher'. From *A Manuscript of Tashrih Al-Aqvam, an Account of the Origins and Occupations of Some of the Sects, Castes and Tribes of India*, by Col. James Skinner, India, 1825

A Meal in Abyssinia

At last supper arrived; first a basket contained half-
a-dozen great rounds of native bread, a tough,
clammy substance closely resembling crepe rubber
in appearance; then two earthenware jugs, one of
water, the other of *talla* – a kind of thin, bitter beer;
then two horns of honey, but not of honey as it is
understood at Thame: this was the product of wild
bees, scraped straight from the tree; it was a greyish
colour, full of bits of stick and mud, bird dung,
dead bees, and grubs. Everything was first carried to
the *abuna* for his approval, then to us. We expressed
our delight with nods and more extravagant smiles.
The food was laid before us and the bearers retired.
At this moment the Armenian shamelessly deserted
us, saying that he must go and see after his boy.

The three of us were left alone, smiling over our
food in the half darkness. In the corner lay our
hamper packed with Irene's European delicacies. We
clearly could not approach them until our host left
us. Gradually the frightful truth became evident that
he was proposing to dine with us.

I tore off a little rag of bread and attempted to eat it.
'This is a very difficult situation,' said the professor;

'I think, perhaps, it would be well to simulate ill-health,' and, holding his hands to his forehead, he began to rock gently from side to side, emitting painfully subdued moans... presently the professor held his stomach and retched a little; then he lay on his back, breathing heavily with closed eyes; then he sat up on his elbow and explained in eloquent dumb show that he wished to rest. The *abuna* understood perfectly, and, with every gesture of sympathy, rose to his feet and left us.

In five minutes, when I had opened a tinned grouse and a bottle of lager and the professor was happily mumbling a handful of ripe olives, the Armenian returned. With a comprehensive wink, he picked up the jug of native beer, threw back his head, and, without pausing to breathe, drank a quart or two. He then spread out two rounds of bread, emptied a large quantity of honey into each of them, wrapped them together, and put them in his pocket. *Moi, je puis manger comme abyssin*, he remarked cheerfully, winked at the grouse, wished us good night, and left us.

EVELYN WAUGH
When the Going was Good

There Were No Table-napkins:
a Gastronomic Fantasy

And now for a party in Morocco. The company is more exalted this time. We were the guests of a distinguished sheikh. We sat on exquisite rugs woven in the villages on the foothills of the Atlas. A sort of janissary stood behind the sheikh during the whole meal. He was quite human, but he did not twitch an eyelash. He could give the Horse Guards a lesson in immobility.

We were attended by three coal-black negresses, consummate creatures. So silent were these, too, that you might have thought them marionettes, excepting that they did not creak. At the beginning of the meal and between courses, one negress held out a brass basin for us to hold our arms out over it. The second poured scented warm water on our hands from a brass ewer. The third featly wiped our hands. Dish succeeded dish in bewildering opulence, set down between us, in great straw containers usually. There were no forks. We thrust with our hands into odorous hills of *couscous*, or with our fingers stripped delicate ribbons of fish from the bones. But the *chef-d'oeuvre* was a dish of mutton and whole onions stewed in honey. I repeat: stewed in honey. It was celestial.

If you are sceptical, go to Morocco for yourself; try it, and you will believe. But remember to be very gracious when your host, the sheikh, explores the hot depths of the stew with his fingers and hands over to you some particularly succulent morsel. And remember there are roast quail to follow, stuffed with raisins and red peppers. Your host in his courtesy and against his principles will offer you beer. But it were pleasanter to join him in a tumbler of sweet tea, one-third filled with mint leaves.

LOUIS GOLDING
Wine and Food, 4

'Chuck out those – they're harmless.'

ANOTHER MAN'S POISON

Domestic food is wholesome, though
'tis homely, And foreign dainties
poisonous, though tasteful.

SIR WALTER SCOTT

No Pie for Me, Please

Away back in '54 when commercial telly got cracking, we were kept busy making film visuals for advertisers sharpening their hooks for an eager public.

Ours was a pocket-size affair, and the living room of my house did duty as studio and, later, projection room when the rushes came back from the labs.

One day the room would be bodged up to resemble a doctor's consulting room where a grey-haired physician warned sternly of the dangers of neglected constipation. A few hours later, the whole place had been turned into the forecourt of a garage where the same grey-haired physician (now magically changed into a mechanic) proclaimed the virtues of some viscous-looking lubricating oil.

It was all great fun except, perhaps, for my wife and for Granny, who lived with us in those distant days. Granny, by the way, although well over eighty, had the appetite of a strapping schoolgirl.

The big day came when Superclient from an

Bakers at work. Opaque watercolour taken from the *Album of Kashmiri Trades*, 1850-60

An Interesting scene, on board an East Indiaman, s

Caricature and engraving of 'An interesting scene on board an East
by George Cruikshank (1792–1878), London, 1818

ing the *Effects of a* **heavy Lurch,** *after dinner.*

Indiaman showing the effects of a heavy lunch – after dinner',

Open Apple Tart.

Galette.

Iced Pudding.

Apricot Fritters.

Pancakes & Apricot Jam.

Charlotte Russe.

Macaroni Cheese.

Cherry Tart.

Mince Pies.

Almond Puddings.

Tartlets.

Compote of Fruits.

Fruit Pudding.

Fruit Tart.

Christmas Plum Pudding.

Milk Pudding.

Roly Poly Jam Pudding.

PUDDINGS & PASTRY.

advertising agency announced he was coming along to direct a filmlet boosting Lemon Meringue Pie...

All was bustle at the studio. The garage scene was struck and, in a trice, appeared a tastefully laid table. Everything sparkled; the cloth was snowy-white; the cutlery gleamed; the napery was impeccable...

Meanwhile, in the kitchen, my wife battled with the lemon meringue pie. As this delicacy was to be photographed only, she permitted herself great liberties in its construction. A sodden clag of dough provided the basis of structure and the formality of cooking was omitted. On top of this she poured grudging froth of an egg-white and browned it lightly in the oven. The whole nonsense was then garnished with slivers of runner-bean in economical lieu of angelica.

'How does it look?'

I held to my eye the neutral-density filter from which no ace cameraman is ever parted.

'Lousy!' I barked. 'Just lousy! Lacks colour! No tonal values! Won't register on pan stock! TED! Listen Ted,' I said urgently, 'Nip round to the corner

Puddings and pastry, from *Mrs Beeton's Book of Household Management*, 1849

shop and get a small tin of brown plastic paint. Tell 'em I'll pay at the week-end without fail.'

We flimped up the anaemic crust of the pie until it looked mouthwateringly crisp and, suddenly, Superclient arrived, bringing with him the groomed young man who was to play the part of the husband sampling his wife's masterpiece.

'It's like this,' explained Superclient tersely, 'our clients make just that thing that turns the simplest lemon meringue pie into a real smasher. I've brought a jingle with me; think your daughter could help us out?'

(I should explain that Ann spent several years at the Guildhall School of Music struggling with the intricacies of Bach, Beethoven... and various other fuddy-duddies quite unknown in the world of advertising.)

Ann examined the masterpiece. 'H'm. Could do, maybe.' She read the words aloud, tapping the rhythm on the lid of the piano ...

'For ting and tang
Choose lemon-meringue
All frothy and feathery whi-ite!

It's as light as a dream
And made with fresh cre-eem …'

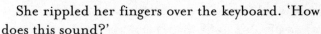

She rippled her fingers over the keyboard. 'How does this sound?'

Superclient nodded his head. 'Roger! Got it, son?'

The young man nodded confidently. 'Yup!' From now on it was all strict filming technique …

All was disciplined efficiency. The young man plunged his spoon into the horrible pudding and then waved it in time with the words. Superclient beat the rhythm with a folded newspaper. Ann bashed away at the piano. Ted grabbed a light…

'No, *no*, NO!' shouted Superclient after half a dozen attempts. 'It stinks! You're supposed to be *enjoying* the stuff so much that you're singing about it.' He glanced at his watch. 'Half-past twelve, damme, let's go and find a drink and then have some lunch.'

And so we left everything just as it was; the elaborately laid table; the camera; the lights on their rickety stands; the pie. Only Granny remained in her quiet sitting room. Fuss and noise, she always said, gave her the jimjams.

Quarter of an hour after chucking-out time we

all came trooping back... and stood speechless in the doorway leading to the studio.

The table was bare and newly polished. All the photographic junk had been stacked neatly in a corner. By the fire sat Granny and on her face was the expression of a cat who has just had a whole Scotch salmon to itself ...

'Well, it was kind of you young people to lay me such a lovely meal... you may think me an awfully greedy girl but I just couldn't resist that pie... I ate every single mouthful...'

The smile of a gourmet spread across her face, 'And I've been such a good girl, too. I've done all the washing-up and put all your nasty photo things away in the corner...'

I snatched up the telephone and dialled furiously.

'Let me know how she gets on,' reassured the voice 'but I should imagine that with all that farinaceous matter the slightly toxic qualities of the paint...'

Since that day it has always been biscuits-and-cheese for me. Somehow I just cannot look a lemon-meringue pie in the face.

GORDON CATLING

An Epicurean Treat

All the inhabitants of the valley treated me with great kindness; but as to the household of Marheyo, with whom I was now permanently domiciled, nothing could surpass their efforts to minister to my comfort. To the gratification of my palate they paid the most unwearied attention. They continually invited me to partake of food, and when after eating heartily I declined the viands they continued to offer me, they seemed to think that my appetite stood in need of some piquant stimulant to excite its activity.

In pursuance of this idea, old Marheyo himself would hie him away to the seashore by the break of day, for the purpose of collecting various species of rare seaweed; some of which among these people are considered a great luxury. After a whole day spent in this employment, he would return about nightfall with several cocoa-nut shells filled with different descriptions of kelp. In preparing these for use he manifested all the ostentation of a professed cook, although the chief mystery of the affair appeared to consist in pouring water in judicious quantities upon the slimy contents of his cocoa-nut shells.

The first time he submitted one of these saline salads to my critical attention I naturally thought that anything collected at such pains must possess peculiar merits; but one mouthful was a complete dose; and great was the consternation of the old warrior at the rapidity with which I ejected his Epicurean treat.

How true it is, that the rarity of any particular article enhances its value amazingly. In some part of the valley — I know not where, but probably in the neighbourhood of the sea — the girls were sometimes in the habit of procuring small quantities of salt, a thimble-full or so being the result of the united labours of a party of five or six employed for the greater part of the day. This precious commodity they brought to the house, enveloped in multitudinous folds of leaves; and as a special mark of the esteem in which they held me, would spread an immense leaf on the ground, and dropping one by one a few minute particles of the salt upon it, invite me to taste them.

From the extravagant value placed upon the article, I verily believe, that with a bushel of common Liverpool salt, all the real estate in Typee might have been purchased. With a small pinch of it in one hand, and a quarter section of a bread-fruit in the other, the greatest chief in the valley would have laughed at all the luxuries of a Parisian table.

HERMAN MELVILLE
Typee

THE IDEAL CUISINE

The ideal cuisine should display an individual character; it should offer a menu judiciously chosen from the kitchen-workshops of the most diverse lands and peoples — a menu reflecting the master's alert and fastidious taste.

NORMAN DOUGLAS
An Almanac

There was an Old Person of Ewell,
Who chiefly subsisted on gruel;
But to make it more nice,
He inserted some mice,
Which refreshed that Old Person of Ewell.

EDWARD LEAR

Heads Were an Extra

My meditations were interrupted by a shout informing the whole camp that dinner was ready. I have sat down to many a barbaric feast among Eskimos in my time, but I have never seen anything to equal this. Only the elders used knives, the younger members of the party simply tore the meat from the bones in the same voracious fashion which we may imagine to have been the custom of our earliest ancestors. Besides the two caribou, a number of heads had been cooked, and one was served out to each member of our party. The heads were an extra, and we were allowed to keep them till after, to eat in our own tent, on condition that none of the leavings should under any circumstances be touched by women or dogs. The muzzle especially was regarded as sacred meat, which must not be defiled.

Then came dessert; but this was literally more than we could swallow. It consisted of the larvae of the caribou fly, great fat maggoty things served up

'Carrots', from *Album Benary* by Ernst Benary, 1876

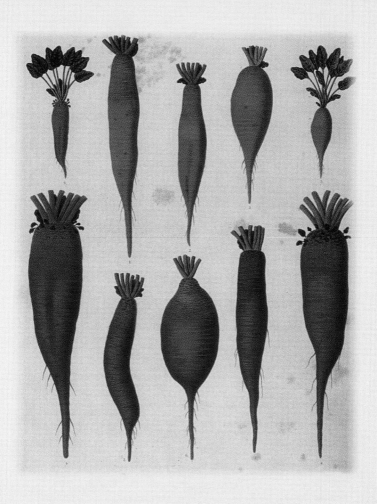

raw just as they had been picked out from the skin of the beasts when shot. They lay squirming on a platter like a tin of huge gentles, and gave a nasty little crunch under the teeth, like crushing a black-beetle.

Ingjugarjuk, ever watchful, noted my embarrassment and observed kindly: 'No one will be offended if you do not understand our food; we all have our different customs.' But he added a trifle maliciously: 'After all, you have just been eating caribou meat; and what are these but a sort of little eggs nourished on the juices of that meat?'

KNUD RASMUSSEN
Across Arctic America

Fun and games at Christmas, from *The Graphic*, November 1874. Caption reads: 'C-c-call tomorrow if you please', to which the medicine bottle responds ,'A teaspoonful every 2 hours'

MUSICAL JACK

After a brief interview, they politely invited me to partake of the supper… they considered themselves peculiarly fortunate in having procured an excellent dish — in fact, a great delicacy — in a place where they expected to meet with but indifferent fare. What this great delicacy was, they did not attempt to explain; and… I felt no inclination to make any further inquiries.

When the hour of supper arrived, the principal dish and, indeed, almost the only one upon the table appeared to me to be a dish of good-sized eels, fried. I being the guest of my new acquaintances had the honour of being the first served with a plate of what the person who presided called 'Musical Jack'. 'Musical Jack', thought I, is some species of eels peculiar to the Mississippi and its tributary waters; and taking it for granted that it was all right, I forthwith began to ply my knife and fork.

'Stop,' said the individual that occupied the bottom of the table, before I had swallowed two mouthfuls. 'You, sir, have no idea, I presume, what you are eating; and since you are our guest for the time being, I think it but right that you should have no cause hereafter to think yourself imposed upon. The dish before you, which we familiarly call 'Musical Jack', is composed of rattlesnakes, which the hunter who accompanies us in our tour of exploration was so fortunate to procure for us this afternoon. It is far from the first time that we have fared thus; and, although our own hunter skinned, decapitated, and dressed the creatures, it was only through dint of coaxing that our hostess was prevailed upon to lend her frying-pan for so vile a purpose.'

Although curiosity had on many occasions prompted me to taste strange and unsavoury dishes, I must confess that never before did I feel such a loathing and disgust as I did towards the victuals before me. I was scarcely able to listen to the conclusion of this short address, ere I found it prudent to hurry out of the room; nor did I return till supper was over...

PETER LUND SIMMONDS
The Curiosities of Food of The Dainties and Delicacies of Different Nations Obtained from the Animal Kingdom (1859)

Guatemalan Food

But you must now notice especially one flower, that here is bought either for decoration or to be eaten. This is the yucca; large spikes, clustering spires of cup-like blossom, creamy and green, ivory and white. The petals, cool, crisp and aromatic, of these flowers, sprinkled with their golden centres shredded over them, dressed with oil and vinegar and rubbed with garlic, form one of the usual dishes of this country. Texture and flavour are both excellent. The stalk is then cooked and eaten as a vegetable, but to me, though I seldom recognized what it was until I enquired, it seemed always rather tasteless and pithy, with a suggestion of soft wood and badly cooked root vegetables ... I cannot say whether these yuccas, though they look precisely the same, only larger and more florescent, are identical with those grown in English gardens, and I have not dared to find out empirically.

Passing on, you reach a court devoted to the sale of Guatemalan blankets, and, beyond it, another that displays embroidered shirts for men and shawls and scarves for women. In its turn, this leads into a colossal sunny *plaza* where the native pottery is to be bought, mounds of earthenware pots and jars, their shape, the perfection of their irreproachable line, seeming more Greek than Spanish, a remark even more applicable to the neigbouring collections of flat dishes, made of an earthenware that is almost rose-coloured, which are used for cooking *tortillas*. Indeed, these large, flat, round plates resemble the discs of the *Discobolus*, so suave and stream-lined are they. From the next immense court, over which hangs a mantle of dust, issues that mingled lowing, bleating and squealing which you have already remarked.

Here, among the young pink porkers on string leads, who so resolutely make an inevitably ineffectual dash for freedom upon their short, apparently unjointed legs, here among the tufted calves attempting to escape, and indeed perhaps the cause of the general frantic behaviour of the animal world — sits a woman with a large round linen basket full of the strangest cattle, the greatest living delicacy of the land: iguanas. These giant lizards, three or four feet long, are tied, like whitings upon an English breakfast-table, or the symbol of eternity, mouth to tail. Otherwise they would thresh out with their tails, which are spiked and can inflict formidable injuries. Their jaws, too, are bound together to prevent their snapping at and biting their prospective devourers, already bargaining over their bodies. Incidentally, the customers cannot poke them in the ribs in the same manner in which they prod the calves and small pigs, to see if they are fat, because, even if an iguana possesses ribs — and at this point my knowledge of reptilian anatomy breaks down — the knobs and spikes of its armour would defeat prying fingers. Weight alone is the criterion.

A clean feeder, the creature lives in the tree-tops of the steaming jungles on sea-level, and subsists on the green leaves round it. The iguana-catcher is trained to net his prey, a difficult profession that needs a long schooling in these swamps and forests; or again, it may be shot — sitting, I apprehend — and in these tropical regions 'a day's iguana shooting' is a popular sport, comparable to 'a day's partridge shooting' here ...

Now it may be that the iguana is no pleasant object to look at. Its small eyes, pail-shaped snout and shark-like jaws, lined with a saw's teeth of steel, are, I know, repellent to many. Even the reptile's best friends, indeed, will be obliged to admit that at first sight it presents a somewhat case-hardened exterior, and that its saurian countenance bears an unpleasing expression, both sarcastic and ferocious. But it is good, *very good*, to eat: and its cost does not amount to more than the equivalent of a shilling; two facts which must tell in its favour.

The ways of cooking it are many, but the best seemed to me to be roast saddle, cooked with herbs, and served in a circle of its own eggs with a rich brown sauce, flavoured with Madeira or port. The saddle is white and tender as the best capon, and the eggs, too, are a suitable, and even delicious, concomitant, once you have grown accustomed to the idea of them.

SIR OSBERT SITWELL
Sing High! Sing Low!

EXPLORER'S DIET

October 8, [1853] Sunday. 'When I was out in the *Advance*, with Captain de Haven, I satisfied myself that it was a vulgar prejudice to regard the liver of the bear as poisonous. I ate of it freely myself, and succeeded in making it a favourite dish with the mess. But I find to my cost that it may sometimes be more savoury than safe. The cub's liver was my supper last night, and to-day I have the symptoms of poison in full measure — vertigo, diarrhoea, and their concomitants.'

I may mention, in connection with the fact which I have given from my journal that I repeated the experiment several times afterward, and sometimes, but not always, with the same result. I remember once, near the Great Glacier, all our party sickened after feeding on the liver of a bear that we had killed; and a few weeks afterward, when we were tempted into a similar indulgence, we were forced to undergo the same penance. The animal in both cases was old and fat. The dogs ate to repletion, without injury.

Another article of diet, less inviting at first, but which I found more innocuous, was the rat. We had failed to exterminate this animal by our varied and perilous efforts of the year before, and a well-justified fear forbade our renewing the crusade. It was marvellous, in a region apparently so unfavourable to reproduction, what a perfect warren we soon had on board. Their impudence and address increased with their numbers. It became impossible to stow anything below decks. Furs, woollens, shoes, specimens of natural history, everything we disliked to lose, however little valuable to them, was gnawed into and destroyed. They harboured among the men's bedding in the forecastle, and showed such boldness in fight and such dexterity in dodging missiles, that they were tolerated at last as inevitable nuisances. Before the winter ended I avenged our griefs by decimating them for my private table.

ELISHA KENT KANE
Arctic Exploration in Search of Sir John Franklin (1898)

DESERT ISLAND DISHES

There is no love sincerer than
the love of food.

BERNARD SHAW

High Living Alone

July 28 was exceptionally fine. The wind from the northwest was light and the air balmy. I overhauled my wardrobe, and bent on a white shirt against nearing some coasting-packet with genteel folk on board. I also did some washing to get the salt out of my clothes. After it all I was hungry, so made a fire and very cautiously stewed a dish of pears and set them carefully aside, till I had made a pot of delicious coffee, for both of which I could afford sugar and cream. But the crowning dish of all was a fish-hash, and there was enough of it for two. I was in good health again, and my appetite was simply ravenous. While I was dining I had a large onion over the double lamp stewing for luncheon later in the day. High living to-day!

JOSHUA SLOCUM
Sailing Alone Round the World

OPENING OYSTERS

While we were thus talking, Jack had been vainly endeavouring to open an oyster with his large knife. 'Here is a simpler way', said I, placing an oyster on the fire; it immediately opened. 'Now', I continued, 'who will try this delicacy?' All at first hesitated to partake of them, so unattractive did they appear. Jack, however, tightly closing his eyes and making a face as though about to take medicine, gulped one down. We followed his example, one after the other, each doing so rather to provide himself with a spoon than with any hope of cultivating a taste for oysters. Our spoons were now ready, and gathering round the pot we dipped them in, not, however, without sundry scalded fingers. Ernest then drew from his pocket the large shell he had procured for his own use, and scooping up a good quantity of soup he put it down to cool, smiling at his own foresight.

JOHANN RUDOLF WYSS
The Swiss Family Robinson

Five Months Solitary

More than a year has passed since the incidents occurred which are the subject of this chapter. During that time much of the detail has faded from my memory, the impressions have become blurred, and the ideas which then formed themselves in my mind are now forgotten. Yet it may be that a few notes on that time spent on the Greenland Ice Cap will be of some use to travellers who, in the future, may be faced with a similar problem. If I, by these notes, can do something to dispel the strange ideas of danger and risk in leaving a man in such a situation, I shall feel justified. There are many men, trappers and the like, who live by themselves for most of the year. An accident is very rare among these men, nor are their minds usually deranged.

The following is a bare outline, from memory, and from an irregular diary, of my five months alone at the Ice Cap Station.

The total provisions at the Station at this time were, including the supplies brought by our party:

6 ration boxes
2 bottles concentrated lemon juice

26 gallons paraffin

1 bottle cod-liver oil

…The food situation was also becoming interesting about this time (March). When I first took over the Station I had, of course, to decide on the scale of rations of food and fuel I was going to keep to, and for this purpose it was necessary to estimate a date of relief. One way would be to choose the latest-possible date, which would allow a very small ration indeed, with the probability of a large amount of supplies being left over. This would have been the safest course, but for various reasons I did not take it. In the first place I did not like rationing. I prefer, in fact, to eat my cake rather than have it. *Carpe Diem* was a tag which served as an excuse whenever I felt hungry. Another reason was that I needed a large amount of fuel to begin with for drying clothes and for reading. I therefore assumed March 15th as the date of relief, and scaled my rations to last till then, leaving a small amount of the less palatable necessities, and a bare allowance of fuel for cooking after that.

It was, therefore, all according to plan when stores began to run out. The paraffin supply especially got short, owing to leakage. This was very tiresome, since I had to spend more and more time in the dark and the house got considerably colder without the lamp to give heat. The food problem solved itself, since one's appetite becomes very small if one takes no exercise, and an allowance of half a pound a day proved ample towards the latter part of my stay.

...By the middle of April there was no more light, luxuries had run out, and the comfort of the house was much reduced. Tobacco was completely exhausted, so tea was used as a substitute. Food consisted of a little oatmeal, just warmed up for breakfast, and thereafter, uncooked pemmican, biscuit and margarine. The most unpleasant part was the frozen condensed moisture which covered the whole inside of the tent, and, hanging down in long icicles from the roof, used to drop off in one's face. It also condensed inside my sleeping-bag, and so froze up any part of it that I was not in contact with.

The Adventures of Henry, by Carl Anderson. Illustration from a cigarette card produced by Kensitas, J.Wix & Sons

Henry

CARL ANDERSON

I tried various substitutes for light; paper, string, ski-wax, etc. None of them was satisfactory, though a lamp made of string in a tin of ski-wax was the best, and would last a few minutes if carefully tended.

… On May 5th the primus gave its last gasp. A few minutes later an extraordinary scraping and scratching sound was heard overhead, which turned out to be the relief party.

AUGUST COURTAULD

'Five Months at the Ice Cap Station' in *Northern Lights: The Official Account of the British Arctic Air-Route Expedition, 1930–1*

IN PRAISE OF TURTLE

Of all the things I ever swallow
Good, well-dressed turtle beats them hollow
It almost makes me wish, I vow,
To have two stomachs, like a cow.

THOMAS HOOD

A royal ascetic sits on a tiger-skin next to a fire, surrounded by offerings of fruit and vases of narcissus. Opaque watercolour, c.1660

Seal Steaks and Soot

Seal meat is coarse and black and sometimes it has a sickeningly oily taste which catches you suddenly unawares and which I think is quite loathsome. Penguin meat is much the same but it plays a straighter game. It does not catch you unexpectedly with a revolting mouthful.

In the *Discovery II* we often killed seals towards the end of the season when the meat supplies were running low. We hung the black carcasses in the rigging. 'Seal steak, sir!' but nearly always I and several others either delicately left ours on the plates or found ourselves suddenly with an unpleasant mouthful and were compelled, much less delicately, to eject it. But somehow, under the pram upon our wind-swept beach, we lost our sense of taste. Manna from heaven could not have seemed more delicious than lumps of seal or penguin meat made into a hash with a handful of oatmeal.

We had two meals a day, two plates of stew each, cooked by old Jock Matheson in the huge, faithful and satisfying saucepan, sooty and heavy and broad-based for an old-fashioned kitchen range. The saucepan sat somewhat precariously upon an iron brazier which the guardian angel of one or other of us had left in the after peak of the *Rapid*. George found it there, lying upon its side under buckets and coils of rope, and brought it ashore. It stood proudly on three legs in an iron tray.

We started the fire in the brazier with slivers of wood damped with paraffin, and then hung little squares of seal blubber over the embers on a frame of twisted wire. The blubber melted and dripped with a crackle on to the embers below. The drips burnt with a bright smoky flame that stank and sent up a hovering cloud of little black smuts. As Matheson stirred his cooking pot over this smelly greasy little altar, he lifted it from time to time so that one of us, sitting nearby, could drop on to the fire a chunk of blubber with our hands or with a sharp splint of wood. Sometimes the chunk of blubber missed the wire frame on which we meant to drop it and fell into the brazier. When that happened it was liable to put the fire out and we would have to light it again. This was at first just a nuisance but later it became a continually recurring disaster, for we began to run short of paraffin and matches... When old Matheson cooked the seal hash over the fire the smoke rose and filled his beard and hair with black smuts. It filled ours, too, when we tended it. They hung from our eyebrows and eyelids and we brushed them away, smearing the soot in streaks across our faces.

We kept the fire going all day and all night with chunks of blubber, keeping watches to tend it. Our hands became covered in grease, which we wiped off on our clothes. The bitter smoke stung our eyes and blackened our faces. At night we placed the brazier in the entrance to our shelter and warmed ourselves at its flickering smoky flames as much as we could, sitting over it in turns. It filled the inside of our house with acrid fumes and covered the roof with soot, but its light, dancing on the over-arching timbers of the boat, was a friendly and reassuring thing. It cheered us as we lay with our arms around each other in our quadruple sleeping bag, shivering and fearing to fall asleep because of the horror of waking.

F. D. OMMANNEY
South Latitude

EATING ALONE IN THE ANTARCTIC

Breakfast didn't count. I rarely took more than tea and a whole-wheat biscuit. Lunch was habitually an out-of-the-can affair, consisting usually of tomato juice, Eskimo biscuits, and frequently a cold meat or fish — either corned beef, tongue, or sardines. These I prepared in masterly fashion. But supper, by rights the high spot in an explorer's day, the hot meal toward which a cold and hungry man looks with mounting anticipation — this meal for a while was a daily fiasco.

I have only to close my eyes to witness again the succession of culinary disasters. Consider what my diary designated at The Corn Meal Incident. Into a boiler I dumped what seemed a moderate quantity of meal, added a little water, and stood it on the stove to boil. That simple formula gave birth to a Hydra-headed monster. The stuff began to swell and dry up, swell and dry up, with fearful blowing and sucking noises. All innocently I added water, more water and still more water. Whereupon the boiler erupted like Vesuvius. All the pots and pans within reach couldn't begin to contain the corn meal that overflowed. It oozed over the stove. It spattered the ceiling. It covered me from head to foot. If I hadn't acted resolutely, I might have been drowned in corn meal. Seizing the container in my mitted hands, I rushed it to the door and hurled it far into the food tunnel. There it continued to give off deadly golden lava until the cold finally stilled the crater.

There were other disasters of the same order. There was the Dried Lima Beans Incident of April 10th ('It's amazing,' the diary reports soberly, 'how much water lima beans can absorb, and how long it takes them to cook. At supper time I had enough half-cooked lima beans to feed a ship's company.') My first jelly dessert bounded like a rubber ball under my knife; the flapjacks had to be scraped from the pan with a chisel. ('And you, the man who sat at a thousand banquets,' goes the accusing entry of April 12th.) I dreaded banquets before I went to Advance Base; and I have come to dread them since. But in April's dark hours I ransacked my memory, trying to remember what they were like. All that I could recall was *filet mignon* spiced and darkened to the colour of an old cavalry boot; or lobster thermidor; or squabs perched on triangles of toast; or chicken salad heaped on billowing lettuce. All these were far beyond the simple foods in my larder. When I did experiment, the results filled the shack with pungent burning smells and coated the skillets with awful gummy residues. But in spite of the missing cookbook, the record was not one of unmitigated failure. Resolved to make a last stand, I took the surviving chicken, hung it for two days from a nail over the stove to thaw, boiled it all in one day, seasoned it with salt and pepper, and served. The soup, which was an unexpected by-product, was delicious; that night I broached a bottle of cider and drank a toast to Escoffier.

ADMIRAL RICHARD BYRD
Alone

FOOD FOR THE GODS

The ridge continued as before. Giant cornices on the right, steep rock slopes on the left. I went on cutting steps on the narrow strip of snow. The ridge curved away to the right and we had no idea where the top was. As I cut around the back of one hump, another higher one would swing into view. Time was passing and the ridge seemed never-ending. In one place, where the angle of the ridge had eased off, I tried cramponing without cutting steps, hoping this would save time, but I quickly realized that our margin of safety on these steep slopes at this altitude was too small, so I went on step-cutting. I was beginning to tire a little now. I had been cutting steps continuously for two hours, and Tenzing, too, was moving very slowly. As I chipped steps around still another corner, I wondered rather dully just how long we could keep it up. Our original zest had now quite gone and it was turning more into a grim struggle. I then realized that the ridge ahead, instead of still monotonously rising,

A Javanese grandee and a Dutchman drink wine together. From the *Album of 116 Drawings Made Under the Supervision of Colin Mackenzie* (1754-1821), 1811-13

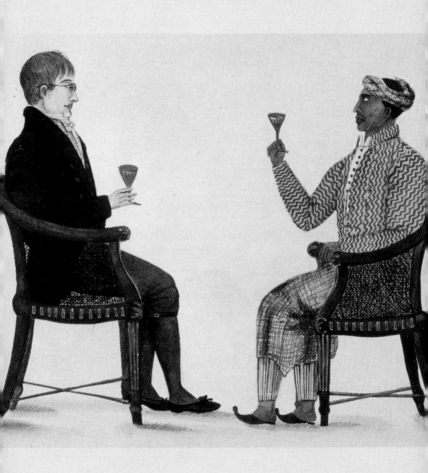

Plate 44

Prickly Pear

London Published as the Act directs by Dr. Thornton & Freeland.

now dropped sharply away, and far below I could see the North Col and the Rongbuk glacier. I looked upwards to see a narrow snow ridge running up to a snowy summit. A few more whacks of the ice-axe in the firm snow and we stood on top.

My initial feelings were of relief — relief that there were no more steps to cut — no more ridges to traverse and no more humps to tantalize us with hopes of success. I looked at Tenzing and in spite of the balaclava, goggles and oxygen mask all encrusted with long icicles that concealed his face, there was no disguising his infectious grin of pure delight as he looked all around him. We shook hands and then Tenzing threw his arm around my shoulders and we thumped each other on the back until we were almost breathless. It was 11.30 a.m. The ridge had taken us two and a half hours, but it seemed like a lifetime. I turned off the oxygen and removed my set. I had carried my camera, loaded with colour film, inside my shirt to keep it warm, so I now

Previous page: Ghazi-al-din Haidar (King of Oudh 1814-27) entertaining Lord and Lady Moira at a banquet in his palace. Opaque watercolour, 1820-2

Pineapple, from *Pomona Britannica; or a Collection of the Most Esteemed Fruits at Present Cultivated in the Country*, by George Brookshaw, London, 1802

produced it and got Tenzing to pose on top for me, waving his axe on which there was a string of flags — United Nations, British, Nepalese and Indian. Then I turned my attention to the great stretch of country lying below us in every direction.

...After some ten minutes of this, I realized that I was becoming rather clumsy-fingered and slow-moving, so I quickly replaced my oxygen set and experienced once more the stimulating effect of even a few litres of oxygen. Meanwhile, Tenzing had made a little hole in the snow and in it he had placed various small articles of food — a bar of chocolate, a packet of biscuits and a handful of lollies. Small offerings, indeed, but at least a token gift to the Gods that all devout Buddhists believe have their home on this lofty summit. While we were together on the South Col two days before, Hunt had given me a small crucifix which he had asked me to take to the top. I, too, made a hole in the snow and placed the crucifix beside Tenzing's gifts.

SIR EDMUND HILLARY
'The Summit' *in The Ascent of Everest by Sir John Hunt*

A MEAL ON MONT BLANC

Our porters left us: a baton was stretched across the room over the stove, and our wet socks and leggings were thrown across it to dry; our boots were placed around the fire, and we set about preparing our evening meal. A pan was placed upon the fire and filled with snow, which in due time melted and boiled; I ground some chocolate and placed it in the pan, and afterwards ladled the beverage into the vessels we possessed, which consisted of two earthen dishes and the metal cases of our brandy flasks. After supper Simond went out to inspect the glacier, and was observed by Huxley, as twilight fell, in a state of deep contemplation beside a crevasse.

Gradually the stars appeared, but as yet no moon. Before lying down we went out to look at the firmament, and I noticed what I suppose has been observed to some extent by everybody, that the stars near the horizon twinkled busily, while those near the zenith shone with a steady light. One large star in particular excited our admiration; it flashed intensely, and changed colour incessantly, sometimes blushing like a ruby, and again gleaming like an emerald. A determinate colour would sometimes remain constant for a sensible time, but usually the flashes followed each other in very quick succession. Three planks were now placed across the room near the stove, and upon these, with their rugs folded round them, Huxley and Hirst stretched themselves, while I nestled on the boards at the most distant end of the room. We rose at eleven o'clock, renewed the fire and warmed ourselves, after which we lay down again. I at length observed a patch of pale light upon the wooden wall of the cabin, which had entered through a hole in the end of the edifice, and rising found that it was past one o'clock. The cloudless moon was shining over the wastes of snow, and the scene outside was at once wild, grand and beautiful.

Breakfast was soon prepared, though not without difficulty — we had no candles, they had been forgotten, but I fortunately possessed a box of wax matches, of which Huxley took charge, patiently igniting them in succession and thus giving us a tolerably continuous light. We had some tea, which had been made at the Montanvert, and carried to the Grandes Mulets in a bottle. My memory of that tea is not pleasant; it had been left a whole night in contact with its leaves, and smacked strongly of tannin. The snow-water, moreover, with which we diluted it was not pure, but left a black residuum at the bottom of the dishes in which the beverage was served. The few provisions deemed necessary being placed in Simond's knapsack, at twenty minutes past two o'clock we scrambled down the rocks, leaving Huxley behind us.

JOHN TYNDALL
The Glaciers of the Alps (1860)

'Of course, we really only bother with Christmas
for the child's sake.'

MEALS TO FORGET

A dessert without cheese is like a
beautiful woman who has lost an eye.

BRILLAT-SAVARIN

Dinner was Soon Over

They were walking back very leisurely; Martin arm-in-arm with Mr Jefferson Brick, and the major and the colonel side-by-side before them; when, as they came within a house or two of the major's residence, they heard a bell ringing violently. The instant this sound struck upon their ears, the colonel and the major darted off, dashed up the steps and in at the street-door (which stood ajar) like lunatics; while Mr Jefferson Brick, detaching his arm from Martin's, made a precipitate dive in the same direction, and vanished also.

'Good Heaven!' thought Martin. 'The premises are on fire! It was an alarm bell!' But there was no smoke to be seen, nor any flame, nor was there any smell of fire. As Martin faltered on the pavement, three more gentlemen, with horror and agitation depicted in their faces, came plunging wildly round the street corner, jostled each other on the steps; struggled for an instant; and rushed into the house,

'A Very Rough Cruise', from *Punch*, May 1933. Caption reads 'And ye're quite certain there's no allowance at the end o' the cruise for meals ye dinna tak...?'

Marmaduke Jones, in Paris for Christmas, finds himself one evening towards the end of his stay almost penniless. Repeated remittances will not arrive until the

morning. A solitary half-crown stands between him and starvation. He selects a cheap restaurant and interviews a waiter as to how he may dine for that sum.

The dinner promises to be excellent, but, alas, in reaching across the table for a knife, poor Jones lays a greater weight upon it than it can bear. One leg gives way with a report like a pistol, and the ruin is complete. The other diners turn in

amazement in time to see Jones saving a solitary cutlet from the wreck of his half-crown dinner

And this into the upset. Arguments, explanations, and expostulations avail nothing without cash to make good the damage. His accusation that it was an accident is scoffed at. His poverty is derided. The crowd which assembles looks upon him as

a malefactor caught redhanded. The strong arm of the law lays hold of him, and Marmaduke Jones spends his last night in Paris in prison.

THE HALF-CROWN DINNER AND THE WEAK-KNEE'D TABLE

DRAWN BY A. GUILLAUME

a confused heap of arms and legs. Unable to bear it any longer, Martin followed. Even in his rapid progress he was run down, thrust aside, and passed by two more gentlemen, stark mad, as it appeared, with fierce excitement.

'Where is it?' cried Martin breathlessly, to a negro whom he encountered in the passage.

'In a eatin room, sa. Kernell, sa, him kep' a seat 'side himself, sa.'

'A seat!' cried Martin.

'For a dinnar, sa.'

Martin stared at him for a moment, and burst into a hearty laugh; to which the negro, out of his natural good humour and desire to please, so heartily responded, that his teeth shone like a gleam of light. 'You're the pleasantest fellow I have seen yet,' said Martin, clapping him on the back, 'and give me a better appetite than bitters.'

With this sentiment he walked into the dining-

'The Half-Crown Dinner and the Weak-Knee'd Table', by A. Guillaume. In Paris for Christmas, Marmaduke Jones, selects a cheap restaurant, but in reaching for a knife he lays a greater weight on the table than it can bear and is sent to prison for the night. From *The Graphic Christmas Number*, 1897

room and slipped into a chair next the colonel, which that gentleman (by this time nearly through his dinner) had turned down in reserve for him, with its back against the table.

It was a numerous company, eighteen or twenty perhaps. Of these some five or six were ladies, who sat wedged together in a little phalanx by themselves. All the knives and forks were working away at a rate that was quite alarming; very few words were spoken; and everybody seemed to eat his utmost in self-defence, as if a famine were expected to set in before breakfast time to-morrow morning, and it had become high time to assert the first law of nature.

The poultry, which may perhaps be considered to have formed the staple of the entertainment — for there was a turkey at the top, a pair of ducks at the bottom, and two fowls in the middle — disappeared as rapidly as if every bird had had the use of its wings, and had flown in desperation down a human throat. The oysters, stewed and pickled, leaped from their capacious reservoirs, and slid by scores into the mouths of the assembly. The sharpest pickles vanished, whole cucumbers at once, like sugar-plums, and no man winked his eye. Great heaps of indigestible matter melted away as ice before the sun. It was a solemn and awful thing to see. Dyspeptic individuals bolted their food in wedges, feeding, not themselves, but broods of nightmares, who were continually standing at livery within them. Spare men, with lank and rigid cheeks, came out unsatisfied from the destruction of heavy dishes, and glared with watchful eyes upon the pastry.

What Mrs Pawkins felt each day at dinner-time is hidden from all human knowledge. But she had one comfort. It was very soon over.

CHARLES DICKENS
Martin Chuzzlewit

The waiter roars it through the hall:
'We don't give bread with one fish-ball!'

GEORGE MARTIN LANE

An American Tragedy

The average American probably spends more than the average citizen of any other country in the world upon food and drink, but he certainly is less well-nourished than the ordinary peasant class in any part of Europe. To say nothing of the little French bourgeois whose income is half that of a New York elevator boy, and yet feeds far better than a Chicago packing millionaire.

That is indeed a tragedy. To have the opportunity and let it pass. But it can be put right. Not in a day nor even in a generation, but in two or three generations. It cannot be put right, however, until the youths of America are trained to look upon life from a different angle. Their values are mostly wrong. As they speak from the bridge of their noses, probably having never been taught that their chest is their natural sound-box, so they live upon their nerves, instead of their food. Their food is the fuel that charges the accumulators: the nerves — and they drive on the accumulators instead of upon the motor, the one source of power, of health and strength: the belly, that is, the stomach-cum-guts, placed by nature amidships, far enough from the navigating room — the brain — to get its orders clearly and near enough from all organs to supply their requirements with a minimum of delay and a maximum of efficiency.

Of course, your belly must not be your god. You should have no false gods. The average American's gods are speed, shows and sugar. They are the first loves of most children; they are desirable in themselves, and in moderation. They are all very well so long as you cannot or do not care to think. There is no exhilaration comparable to that of speed, nor any greater relaxation than a well-acted play or even film, no surer way to forget one's worries or one's unsatisfactory self. But if it is good to forget sometimes, it is better to remember and to think: to remember others and to think of so many people and so many things so well worth thinking about. To think of others is what matters most, and that is not done on a doped stomach or closed-up bowels; it is not done on ice water any more than on fire water, 'hard liquor'. That is what the new generation needs to be taught in America, and maybe elsewhere as well. Food is a very important matter and so is drink. Too few Americans realize it at present. Too many eat what happens to be at hand, good or bad. It is all the same. They have no time to think about it. They drink iced water when they are thirsty and strong spirits when they want to be gay, that is to say, when they want to forget. Wine is too dear to drink when thirsty, and too weak to get drunk on; and who has time to drink wine, anyway? Nobody.

It is all wrong. They should drink wine, even if it be poor wine and not appealing to their taste, even if it were merely for the sake of taking more time than they do over their meals, as a cure for that pernicious habit of bolting one's food, a crazy habit which ruins the health of millions of people, people who have no idea of what to do with the spare time on their hands and yet swallow a few sandwiches for lunch in five minutes instead of enjoying a proper meal in a rational manner.

ANDRÉ L. SIMON
Wine and Food, 5

AN UNSATISFACTORY VEGETABLE

Time passed slower than ever in our new surroundings and we became painfully aware of hunger and
thirst. My friend the Arab seemed the only possible
source of refreshment. Once again I made my way
over to him, this time rather more cautiously than
before, for things were beginning to warm up
round us, and opened negotiations. The first thing
was to find out where he kept his water supply. It
turned out that there was a well in the sand by the
side of his allotment. Lying on the sand, with the
help of an old leather bucket and a long bit of
string, I managed in a short time to pull up enough
water to fill two large water-bottles. The slimy,
brackish liquid thus produced seemed more
delicious than vintage Champagne…

I next asked him whether he could sell us
anything to eat. Always a man of few words, he
pointed to a bright-green vegetable marrow
growing at his feet. 'Any eggs?' I said. 'No,' he said.
It was only too clear the vegetable marrow was all
that we were going to get; and eventually it changed

hands for a thousand-lire note. It was not cheap, but it was the smallest note I had and one could hardly expect change in the circumstances. Carrying it as proudly as if it had won a prize at the Crystal Palace, I started back to the jeeps by a suitably circuitous route. On the way I filled my pockets with unripe dates off the date palm. We had all the makings of a feast.

We had scarcely sat down to breakfast when a fierce controversy broke out over our *plat de résistance*. My own claim that it was a vegetable marrow was brushed scornfully aside by Sandy, who said that he knew that it was a cucumber. On being told that cucumbers did not grow to that size, he said that anyone who knew anything about vegetables could see that it was a tropical cucumber. Nettled by this I retorted rather unjustly that anyone who knew anything at all could see that he was nothing but a city slicker whose knowledge of the country was derived solely from the low suburban race course which he frequented.

Prolonged lack of food and drink is apt to fray the nerves. Our tempers were not at their best, and we both felt by now that we could have cheerfully used up our remaining strength in fighting each other over the identity of the rather sad-looking vegetable which lay between us, cut up into unappetizing green slices already covered with sand and flies. Fortunately a breach of the peace was avoided thanks to Sergeant Seekings, the only real agricultural expert of the party, who drew the fire of both parties by suggesting that the object of our controversy must be a kind of pumpkin, a diagnosis so manifestly outrageous that Sandy and I sank our differences in a united but entirely unsuccessful attempt to persuade Seekings that he was talking nonsense. Not long after eating it, whatever it was, we were all attacked by the most violent stomach ache. Altogether it was an unsatisfactory vegetable.

FITZROY MacLEAN
Eastern Approaches

Taking Water With It

There was the sad case of some dehydrated food which was dropped to us at a stage of the winter when we had run very short indeed of ordinary food. It was the first time that any of us had seen dehydrated food, and the pleasure with which we regarded the first sacks of strange, dried-up looking flakes, variously labelled 'milk', 'mutton', 'eggs', 'carrots', 'onions' and 'potatoes', but all looking strangely alike, was mingled with curiosity and, to some extent, with misgiving. At any rate, before trying them, we read and carried out meticulously the written directions which accompanied them, of which the principal was to soak them in water for twenty-four hours before cooking and eating them. The result was astonishing. On being soaked, the uninteresting looking flakes swelled up to several times their original size and became lumps of meat or slices of vegetable, as the case might be, and we soon found that a judicious mixture of dehydrated mutton, onions and potatoes properly soaked and then baked in Ginger's mother's oven made a very creditable shepherd's pie, an undreamed-of luxury in our rather strained circumstances. Clearly, dehydrated food was just the thing for us, especially as its light weight made it far more easily transportable than tinned food.

Delighted, we immediately signalled for further supplies in order that we might share with the Partisans the benefit of our new discovery. On their arrival, we handed them over to the Quartermaster's department, being careful to add full instructions for their use. But these they brushed aside lightheartedly. 'We know all about that,' they said and started to distribute the sacks to various neighbouring units. We had our doubts, but thought it better not to voice them.

It was only afterwards that we heard what had happened. The dehydrated food had not been soaked but gulped down as it was. This was dry work, or so the Partisans thought, and so they washed it down with copious draughts of water from the neighbouring brook. Then, with disconcerting suddenness, the stuff began to swell inside them until it had reached several times its original dimensions. Their ensuing discomfort was considerable, though not so acute as that of another Partisan, who at about this time ate a stick of plastic high-explosive, mashing it up with milk, under the impression that it was some kind of maize porridge.

FITZROY MACLEAN
Eastern Approaches

JERUSALEM ARTICHOKE

These roots are dressed divers wayes, some boile them in water, and after stew them with sacke and butter, adding a little ginger. Others bake them in pies, putting Marrow, Dates, Ginger, Raisons of the sun, Sacke, etc. Others some other way as they are led by their skill in Cookerie. But in my judgement which way soever they be drest and eaten, they are a meat more fit for a swine, than men.

JOHN GOODYER
Gerard's Herbal (1633)

ON ICE

From New York to New Orleans I have eaten delicacies that have been frozen into almost complete tasteless- ness — strawberries, chicken, asparagus, soft-shelled crabs, all tasting very much the same through too prolonged a sojourn 'on the ice'. This phrase 'on the ice' follows one round the States; it has the same meaning as our 'in the larder', which indeed is what the ice-box has become in most American homes.

When, owing to severe illness, I had to cancel on Saturday morning an engagement for a 'banquet' on the following Monday night, I was told reproachfully that 'the chickens were already on the ice' on the ice three days, with an outside temperature hovering around zero! I should have been more surprised had I not a short while earlier complained at a famous New York restaurant that my chicken was tough and tasteless through being too long on the ice, and heard the waiter reply, 'It's only been on the ice a week.' When I told him that normally the chickens I ate had not been on the ice at all, I expect he thought I was a fool.

In Charleston we enjoyed the negro cooking, because negroes, like Sussex people and myself, are scared of electrical devices. But I found that American visitors to these places did not share our satisfaction. 'I'm disappointed in this negro cookery,' a charming New Yorker said to me.

'I don't think it's at all what it's cracked up to be. We did very much better at Miami where all the food came down by ice train from New York. You ate it straight off the ice.'

SHEILA KAYE-SMITH
Kitchen Fugue

There was an
Old Person whose habits
Induced him to feed upon Rabbits;
When he'd eaten eighteen
He turned perfectly green,
Upon which he relinquished those habits.

EDWARD LEAR

THE INVITATION

To sup with thee thou didst me home invite;
And mad'st a promise that mine appetite
Sho'd meet and tire, on such lautitious meat,
The like not Heliogabalus did eat:
And richer wine wo'dst give to me, thy guest,
Then Roman Sylla powr'd out at his feast.
I came; tis true, and lookt for fowle of price,
The bastard phenix; bird of paradice;
And for no less then aromatick wine
Of maydens-blush, commixt with jessimine.
Cleane was the herth, the mantle larded jet;
Which wanting lar, and smoke, hung weeping wet;
At last, i'th'noone of winter, did appeare
A ragd-soust-neats-foot with sick vineger:
And in a burnisht flagonet stood by
Beere small as comfort, dead as charity.
At which amaz'd and pondering on the food,
How cold it was, and how it child my blood;
I curst the master; and I damn'd the source;
And swore I'de got the ague of the house.
Well, when to eat thou dost me next desire,
I'le bring a fever; since thou keep'st no fire.

ROBERT HERRICK

Bring on the Dancing Girls

We had left all our servants behind at Panjim, and not an iota of our last night's supper had escaped the ravenous maws of the boatmen.

Presently matters began to mend. The old lady recollected that in days of yore she had possessed a pound of tea, and, after much unlocking and rummaging of drawers, she produced a remnant of that luxury. Perseverance accomplished divers other feats, and after about an hour more of half starvation we sat down to a breakfast composed of five eggs, a roll of sour bread, plantains, which tasted exactly like edible cotton dipped in *eau sucrée*, and a 'fragrant infusion of the Chinese leaf' whose perfume vividly reminded us of the haystacks in our native land… Sharp appetites, however, removed all our squeamishness, and the board was soon cleared. The sting of hunger blunted, we lighted our 'weeds', each mixed a cordial portion in a tea-cup, and called aloud for the *nautch*, or dance, to begin.

RICHARD F. BURTON
Goa, and the Blue Mountains (1851)

A miniature calendar scene of feasting and dancing for February, from *The Golf Book*, Simon Bening, Netherlands (Bruges), 1520-30

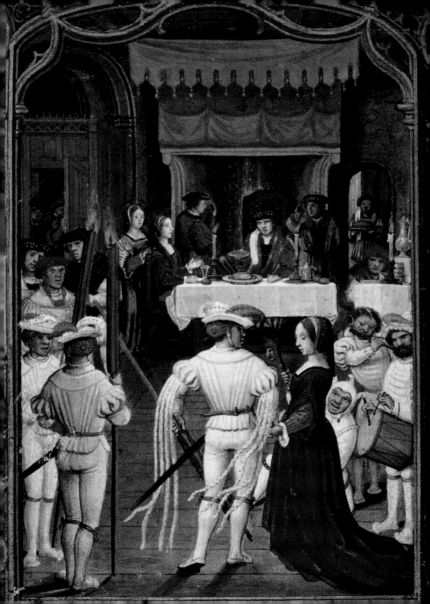

CHEESE.

1—Gorgonzola.　2—Double Gloucester.　3—Koboko.　4—Parmesan.　5—Dutch.
6—Roquefort.　7—Schabzieger.　8—Dunragit.　9—York Cream.　10—Port du Salut.
11—Cheddar.　12—Pommel.　13—Camembert.　14—Mainzer.　15—Cheshire.
16—Stilton.　17—Cream Bondon.　18—Gruyere.　19—Wiltshire Loaf.　20—Cheddar Loaf.

Unfortunate Effects
of Cheese and Plums

Since reaching the islands (the Azores) I had lived most luxuriously on fresh bread, butter, vegetables, and fruits of all kinds. Plums seemed the most plentiful on the *Spray*, and these I ate without stint. I had also a Pico white cheese that General Manning, the American consul-general, had given me, which I supposed to be eaten, and of this I partook with the plums. Alas! by night-time I was doubled up with cramps. The wind, which was already a smart breeze, was increasing somewhat, with a heavy sky to the sou'west. Reefs had been turned out, and I must turn them in again somehow. Between cramps I got the mainsail down, hauled out the earings at best I could, and tied away point by point, in the double reef. There being sea-room, I should, in strict prudence, have made all snug and gone down at once to my cabin. I am a

Cheese. Colour plate from *The Book of Household Management* by Mrs Isabella Beeton, Ward Lock & Co, 1899

careful man at sea, but this night, in the coming storm, I swayed up my sails, which, reefed though they were, were still too much in heavy weather; and I saw to it that the sheets were securely belayed. In a word, I should have laid to, but did not. I gave her the double-reefed mainsail and whole jib instead and set her on her course. Then I went below, and threw myself upon the cabin floor in great pain. How long I lay there I could not tell, for I became delirious.

When I came to, as I thought, from my swoon, I realized that the sloop was plunging into a heavy sea, and looking out of the companionway, to my amazement I saw a tall man at the helm. His rigid hand, grasping the spokes of the wheel, held them as in a vice. One may imagine my astonishment. His rig was that of a foreign sailor, and the large red cap he wore was cockbilled over his left ear, and all was set off with shaggy black whiskers. He would have been taken for a pirate in any part of the world. While I gazed upon his threatening aspect I forgot the storm, and wondered if he had come to cut my throat. This he seemed to divine. 'Señor,' said he, doffing his cap, 'I have come to do you no harm.'

And a smile, the faintest in the world, but still a smile, played on his face, which seemed not unkind when he spoke. 'I have come to do you no harm, I have sailed free,' he said, 'but was never worse than a *contrabandista*. I am one of Columbus's crew,' he continued. 'I am the pilot of the *Pinta* come to aid you. Lie quiet, señor captain,' he added, 'and I will guide your ship to-night. You have a *calentura*, but you will be all right to-morrow.'

I thought what a very devil he was to carry sail. Again, as if he read my mind exclaimed: 'Yonder is the *Pinta* ahead; we must overtake her. Give her sail; give her sail! *Vale, vale muy vale!*' Biting off a large quid of black twist, he said, 'You did wrong, captain, to mix cheese with plums. White cheese is never safe unless you know whence it comes. *Quien sabe*, it may have been from *leche de Capra* and becoming capricious...'

'Avast there!' I cried. 'I have no mind for moralizing.'

JOSHUA SLOCUM
Sailing Alone Round the World

ENGLISH CHEESE

Last summer I was in Cardiff, a city with public buildings which would do credit to a great metropolis. Having taken advice as to the best eating-place, I found myself in a beautifully fitted restaurant where, as at Leicester, the service was performed by waitresses and not by waiters. A truly excellent and inexpensive luncheon wound up with a local dainty in the shape of a small bilberry (or blaeberry, or whortleberry, or whinberry) pudding which had been steamed in a basin not much bigger than a teacup.

A bright hope flashed up within me. Within two leagues of maritime and industrial Cardiff stands the ancient burgh of Caerphilly, with the ruins of a castle as big as Royal Windsor's: and Caerphilly has long been renowned for a very pale cheese, made in cakes not much thicker than the much more modern Italian Bel Paese. It occurred to me that in a restaurant so laudably regional as to serve bilberry (or blaeberry, or whortleberry, or whinberry) puddings made from local fruit, I might expect to find the local cheese. My Hebe, during a long and audible conversation with a sententious client at the next table, had revealed herself as an intelligent young woman; but when I asked for Caerphilly cheese she laughed. She could bring me Cheddar, Camembert, Roquefort, Gorgonzola, and also little wedges of Gruyère wrapped up in silver paper; but not Caerphilly.

I inquired if she had ever heard of Caerphilly. The damsel replied that she 'ought to have', seeing that her father was born there; but when I said 'Surely you know that there is a Caerphilly cheese', she answered saucily that she 'expected there was plenty of cheese in the Caerphilly shops the same as everywhere else'. Thus it dawned on me that Caerphilly was without honour in its own country... I told her that I would be lunching the next day at the same table and that I should look forward to Caerphilly cheese.

The morrow came, but not the cheese. Instead a manager was brought to me who admitted the propinquity of Caerphilly... but added somewhat reproachfully that nobody ever asked for it and that the last time he bought any, most of it went bad.

ERNEST OLDMEADOW
Wine and Food, 1

AVOCADO, OR THE FUTURE OF EATING

One day not long ago in Los Angeles I found myself, banderillas in hand, facing the horns of a dilemma. I had gone into a Corn Exchange bank to exchange some corn and had fallen into conversation with the manager. He was very affable and insisted I inspect the assets of the branch, which included, among other things, the teeth Bryant Washburn had used in his film career.

Issuing into the hot sunlight of the street, I was dismayed to find that it was time for lunch, and since I had forgotten to bring along a bag of pemmican, I would have to eat in Los Angeles — a fairly exact definition of the term 'the kiss of death'. I looked around me. On my left I could obtain a duplexburger and a Giant Malted Milk Too Thick For a Straw; on my right the feature was barbecued pork fritters and orangeade.

Unnerved, I stopped a passing street Arab and courteously enquired where I might find a cheap but clean eating house. Phil the Fiddler (for it was he) directed my steps to a pharmacy bearing the legend 'Best Drug Stores, Inc'. Merely for the record I dined off an avocado sandwich on whole wheat and a lime rickey, and flunked my basal-metabolism test later that afternoon. I don't pretend to blame the management for my physical shortcomings; all I want them to do is laugh off their menu, a copy of which I seem to have before me.

In general 'Soda Fountain Suggestions' (Best Drug Stores, Inc) is an attractively printed job in two colours (three, if you count the gravy), and though it can hardly hope to rival the success of *Gone With the Wind*, I suppose there is an audience which will welcome it. The salads and three-decker sandwiches are treated with a certain gaiety and quaint charm which recall *Alice of Old Vincennes*. The banana splits and hot-and-cold Ovaltines are handled with a glib humour in the text, which is more than I can say for the way they are handled behind the fountain.

The day I was there, a simply appalling oath escaped the lips of one of the dispensers when he dropped some fudge on his shoe. The authors have

included a very disarming foreword short enough to
quote in its entirety.

> *It is our earnest desire to fulfill the name that we
> have chosen for our chain, THE BEST. We can only
> accomplish this by serving you best. Any criticisms or
> suggestions will be appreciated by the management.*

Only a churl would decline so graceful a gambit.
Messieurs en garde!

Specially, gentlemen, my criticism concerns that
cocky little summary of yours at the bottom of the
menu. 'Best Soda Fountains', you proclaim flatly,
'are BEST because: the ice creams contain no
'fillers' (starch, albumen, etc.); the syrups are made
from cane sugar and real fruits; the coffee is a
special blend made the modern Silex way with a
specially filtered water,' and so forth. Let some of
the younger boys in the troop think the millennium
has come to the City of Our Lady, Queen of the

A 'Gastronomic Symphony' or 'Bringing in the
Boar's Head'. From *Punch Almanack*, 1935

Drawn and Engraved by Mr George Cruikshank.

Dick, The Captain, and Squire Jenkin

Dining in the Palais Royal. Dick, 'The Captain and Squire
Jenkin Dining at Henry's, in The Palais Royal'. From *Life in Paris;
comprising the rambles, sprees, and amours of Dick Wildfire... and ... Squire*

Published Jan'y 1.st 1822 by John Fairburn Broadway, Lon

Dining at Verys in the Palais Royal

Jenkins and Captain O'Shuffleton; with the whimsical adventures of the Halibut.
John Fairburn: London, 1822. Illustration by George
Cruikshank, London, 1822

Angels, what are the facts?

In the first place, you needn't think you can woo me with any such tinsel as 'the ice creams contain no 'fillers' (starch, albumen, etc.)'. One thing I'll have in my ice cream or it's no dice and that's fillers. I don't even insist on ice cream as long as I can stuff myself with fillers. You heap my plate with albumen and starch (any kind, even laundry starch) and stand clear. Call me a piggy if you want to, but I just can't get *enough* …

Quite honestly, your statement that the syrups 'are made from cane sugar and real fruits' surprised me. If that's a boast, I must say it's a pretty hollow one. It might interest you to know that back in 1917 the Allied High Command specified *beet* sugar and *false* fruits in all syrups purchased by its commissary department. Didn't know that, did you? Probably too busy evading the draft at the time. Well, you ask any biochemist his recommendation on sugars, as I did recently;

The Earl of Bridgewater and his dogs, seated at a dinner table. Taken from *Historical Studies*, by John Richard Green, Macmillan & co; London, 1903

you'll get the same terse answer: beet sugar and false fruits.

I have this cousin of mine who is a perfect wiz at chemistry — really astonishing marks for a boy of nineteen in high school — and no matter what you ask him, he'll give you the same answers: beet sugar and false fruits. Frankly, the family's getting a little worried about it; they have to keep Benny chained to a ring on the floor most of the time.

Furthermore, it's useless to try to creep into my heart with any blandishments like 'the coffee is a special blend made the modern Silex way with a specially filtered water.' Filtering Los Angeles water robs it of its many nourishing ingredients, not least of which is chow mein. It is an interesting fact, known to anybody who has ever been interned in that city or its suburbs, that the water possesses a rich content of subgum almond chow mein, Cantonese style, and one or two cases have even been reported where traces of peanut candy and lychee nuts were found.

The assertion of a friend of mine that he once saw an Irish houseboy come out of a water faucet, of course, must be regarded as apocryphal. The Irish are a wiry little people, but they are not as wiry as all that. Nor are they ready as yet for self-government which my distinguished opponents, the gentlemen of the affirmative, claim they should have.

And so, honourable judges and ladies and gentlemen, we of the negative conclude that the Irish should not be given independence because

(1) we need them for a coaling station,

(2) there is a high percentage of illiteracy, and

(3) if we do, Ireland will soon be snatching up Gaum or 'chewing Gaum', so to speak.

I thank you.

S. J. PERELMAN
Crazy Like a Fox

FOOD AND FANTASY

Part of the secret of success in life
is to eat what you like and let the food
fight it out inside.

MARK TWAIN

EATING OYSTER

'O Oysters, come and walk with us!'
The Walrus did beseech.
'A pleasant walk, a pleasant talk,
Along the briny beach:
We cannot do with more than four,
To give a hand to each.'

The eldest Oyster looked at him,
But never a word he said:
The eldest Oyster winked his eye,
And shook his heavy head —
Meaning to say he did not choose
To leave the oyster-bed.

But four young Oysters hurried up,
All eager for the treat:
Their coats were brushed, their faces washed,
Their shoes were clean and neat —
And this was odd, because, you know,
They hadn't any feet.
Four other Oysters followed them,

And yet another four;
And thick and fast they came at last,
And more, and more, and more —
All hopping through the frothy waves,
And scrambling to the shore.

The Walrus and the Carpenter
Walked on a mile or so,
And then they rested on a rock
Conveniently low:
And all the little Oysters stood
And waited in a row.

'But not on us!' the Oysters cried,
Turning a little blue.
'After such kindness, that would be
A dismal thing to do!'
'The night is fine,' the Walrus said.
'Do you admire the view?

'The time has come,' the Walrus said,
'To talk of many things:
Of shoes — and ships — and sealing-wax —

Of cabbages — and kings
And why the sea is boiling hot —
And whether pigs have wings.'

'But, wait a bit,' the Oysters cried,
'Before we have our chat;
For some of us are out of breath,
And all of us are fat!'
'No hurry!' said the Carpenter.
They thanked him much for that.

'A loaf of bread,' the Walrus said,
'Is what we chiefly need:
Pepper and vinegar besides
Are very good indeed —
Now if you're ready, Oysters dear,
We can begin to feed.'

'It was so kind of you to come!
And you are very nice!'
The Carpenter said nothing but

Decorative handwritten dinner menu taken from Gap St
Jacques, French Indo-Chinese restaurant, late 19th century

Menu

Potage aux pâtes d'Italie
Poissons sauce crevettes
Timbale milanaise
Filet aux fonds d'artichauts
Petits pois à la française
Aspic de bécassines
Sorbet au champagne
Pintade truffée
Salade d'aréopuer
Asperges à la crème
Bombe glacée
Dessert.

DRAWN BY W.TAYLER ESQ^{RE} BENGAL CIVIL SERVICE.

LITH^D BY J. BOUVIER

THE BREAKFAST.

Published Feby 1st 1842, for the Proprietor by T.Mc Lean 26, Haymarket London.
PRINTED AT THE 26TH LITHC ESTABT 26, HAYMARKET LOND.

'Cut us another slice:
I wish you were not quite so deaf —
I've had to ask you twice!'

'It seems a shame,' the Walrus said,
'To play them such a trick,
After we've brought them out so far,
And made them trot so quick!'
The Carpenter said nothing but
'The butter's spread too thick!'

'I weep for you,' the Walrus said:
'I deeply sympathize.'
With sobs and tears he sorted out
Those of the largest size
Holding his pocket-handkerchief
Before his streaming eyes.

'O Oysters,' said the Carpenter,
'You've had a pleasant run!
Shall we be trotting home again?'

An East India Company civil servant and his wife breakfast-
ing on fried fish, rice and Sylhet oranges. Lithograph by J.
Bouvier. From *Sketches Illustrating the Manner and Customs of the
Indians and the Anglo-Indians* by William Taylor, 1842

But answer came there none
And this was scarcely odd, because
They'd eaten every one.

'I like the Walrus best,' said Alice: 'because, you see, he was a little sorry for the poor oysters.'

'He ate more than the Carpenter, though,' said Tweedledee. 'You see, he held his handkerchief in front, so that the Carpenter couldn't count how many he took: contrariwise.'

'That was mean!' Alice said indignantly. 'Then I like the Carpenter best if he didn't eat so many as the Walrus.'

'But he ate as many as he could get,' said Tweedledum.

LEWIS CARROLL
Through the Looking-Glass

MOONSHINE

The stones of their grapes are exactly like hail; and I am perfectly satisfied that when a storm or high wind in the Moon shakes their vines, and breaks the grapes from the stalks, the stones fall down and form our hail showers. I would advise those who are of my opinion to save a quantity of these stones when it hails next, and make Lunarian wine. It is common beverage at St Luke's. Some material circumstances I had nearly omitted. They put their bellies to the same use as we do a sack, and throw whatever they have occasion for into it, for they can shut and open it again when they please, as they do their stomachs; they are not troubled with bowels, liver, heart, or any other intestines; neither are they encumbered with clothes, nor is there any part of their bodies unseemly or indecent to exhibit.

Original Travels and Surprising Adventures of
Baron Munchausen (1785)

A Nightmare Lunch

An epic lunch – partaken in a dream –
With André Simon and Mr Neame
(Maurice Healy of legal fame
And A. J. Symons also came)
Wines and meats and little fishes
Combined to make delicious dishes
To put before these famous men –
Appended is a list of them.

Bird's-nest soup and hot *hors-d'oeuvre*,
Accompanied by Clicquot (Veuve):
The blending sounds a trifle curious,
Only one guest found it injurious:
Indeed he was so indisposed,
He murmured with his eyes fast closed,
'A this year's bird in last year's nest' –
Then died upon his neighbour's breast.

The chopped-up tails of mountain goats
Pounded with mint and Quaker oats,
Proved a very favourite dish

('Twas handed round before the fish).
The trout was cooked in Corton Blanc –
At least one guest burst into song –
Then oysters from the Apennines
Served with a novel blend of wines

For fear the wine should not go round –
The reasoning was very sound –
A 1919 Montrachet
Was wedded to a *vin du pays*.
From childhood's days we've learnt to know
Rough with the smooth must always go,
The only comment made was 'Reely!'
It came from Mr Maurice Healy.

Sausages (Swiss) with cream and spice,
Garnished with snips of Edelweiss.
Crocodiles' livers, a dainty rare,
Carefully packed and sent 'by air'.
Caviare served with the port,
Oh, surely an unusual thought

Proclaimed a genius was the host,
The subject of a special toast.

Epilogue
The guests retired with thankful hearts,
And even fuller other parts.
They were not seen for many days,
Alas! the gourmet always pays.

BETTY P. METCALFE
Wine and Food, 2

LUNCH WITH AUNT JOBISKA

The Pobble who has no toes
Was placed in a friendly Bark,
And they rowed him back, and carried him up
To his Aunt Jobiska's Park.
And she made him a feast at his earnest wish
Of eggs and buttercups fried with fish; –
And she said, – 'It's a fact that the whole world knows,
'That Pobbles are happier without their toes.'

EDWARD LEAR
The Pobble Who Has No Toes

Lunch with Aunt Jobiska

The Two Old Bachelors

Two old Bachelors were living in one house;
One caught a Muffin, the other caught a Mouse.
Said he who caught the Muffin
to him who caught the Mouse,
'This happens just in time,
for we've nothing in the house,
Save a tiny slice of lemon and
a teaspoonful of honey,
And what to do for dinner,
since we haven't any money?
And what can we expect if we haven't any dinner
But to lose our teeth and eyelashes and keep on
growing thinner?'

Said he who caught the Mouse
to him who caught the Muffin,

(*Top*) Pitt and Napoleon feast upon the world as a plum
pudding. (*Bottom*) Caricature of French General Dumouriez.
Both from *The Caricatures of Gillray* by James Gillray, London, 1818

Overleaf: The dukes of York, Gloucester and Ireland dine with
Richard II. Late 15th-century miniature from *Chronique d'Angleterre*
by Wavrin, Jean de, Seigneur de Forestel, S. Netherlands (Bruges)

The Plumb-pudding in danger – or – State Epicures taking un Petit Souper.

"*the great Globe itself and all which it inherit*" is too small to satisfy such insatiable appetites

DUMOURIER dining in State at St. James's on the 15 May 1793

Er parle dune grant feste

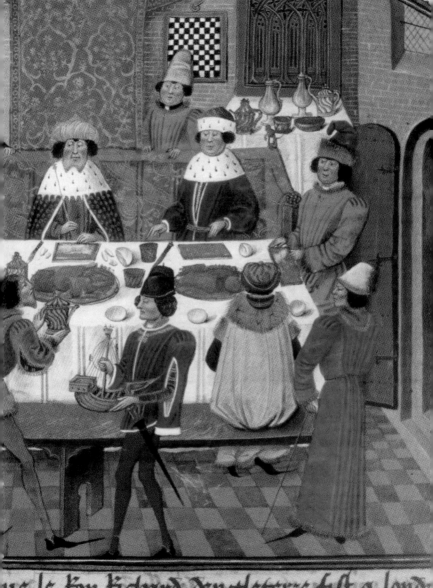

ue le ror richard denoteterre fist a lond

'We might cook this little Mouse
if we only had some Stuffin.'
If we had but Sage and Onion
we could do extremely well,
But how to get that Stuffin' it is difficult to tell.'
Those two old Bachelors ran quickly to the town
And asked for Sage and Onion,
as they wandered up and down.
They borrowed two large Onions,
but no Sage was to be found,
in the Shops or in the Market
or in all the Gardens round.

But someone said, 'A hill there is,
a little to the north,
And to its purpledicular top
a narrow way leads forth;
And there among the rugged rocks
abides an ancient Sage,
An earnest Man, who reads all day
a most perplexing page.

'The Reverend Doctor Syntax and His Spouse at Teatime'.
Colour plate, J. Johnston, Cheapside, London, 1820

Climb up and seize him by the toes,
all studious as he sits,
And pull him down,
and chop him into endless little bits.
Then mix him with your Onion
(cut up likewise into scraps),
And your Stuffin' will be ready,
and very good – perhaps.'

Those two old Bachelors, without loss of time,
The nearly purpledicular crags
at once began to climb;
And at the top among the rocks,
all seated in a nook,
They saw that Sage a-reading
of a most enormous book.
'You earnest Sage!' aloud they cried,
'Your book you've read enough in,
We wish to chop you into bits
and mix you into Stuffin.'

But that old Sage looked calmly up,
and with his awful book
At those two Bachelors' bald heads
a certain aim he took;
And over crag and precipice they rolled
promiscuous down —
At once they rolled, and never stopped
in lane or field or town;
And when they reached their house, they found
(besides their want of Stuffin')
The Mouse had fled and previously had
eaten up the Muffin.

They left their home in silence
by the once convivial door;
And from that hour those Bachelors
were never heard of more.

EDWARD LEAR

THE DREAM

Last night I supped on lobster; it nearly drove me mad
For when at last I got to sleep a funny dream I had.

I dreamed the famous Albert Hall
was turned into a pub,
And there was held a sort of Philharmonic club.
With poets, painters, politicians,
famous statesmen, too,
With actors, authors, clergymen, and ladies not a few.

Chorus
For everyone of them had to sing;
if anyone said: 'I've a cold.'
'Sing or settle for drinks all round,'
they very soon were told.
The Prince of Wales was chairman,
and of course he opened the Ball
And sang the chorus of every song
at the concert in Albert Hall.

When Princess Beatrice rose to sing,
with cheers the building rang,
'I'll never marry if he's got no cash,' she sang.
Then Henry, Prince of Battenburg,
got up and made a bow
And sang in sweet harmonic tones:
'I'm living with mother now.'

Repeat Chorus

Then Dizzy sang 'God Save the Queen',
but Parnell hissed him down,
And Mr Gladstone tried to sing
The Harp without a Crown.
But Chamberlain soon shut him up,
for he sang: 'Not for Joe;'
While Henry Churchill warbled:
'Is it likely? O dear no.'

Repeat Chorus

ANON

FERDINANDO AND ELVIRA, OR
THE GENTLE PIEMAN

At a pleasant evening party
I had taken down to supper
One whom I will call Elvira,
and we talked of love and Tupper,
Mr Tupper and the poets,
very lightly with them dealing,
For I've always been distinguished
for a strong poetic feeling.
Then we let off paper crackers,
each of which contained a motto,
And she listened while I read them,
till her mother told her not to.
Then she whispered, 'To the ball-room
we had better, dear, be walking;
If we stop down here much longer,
really people will be talking.'
There were nobleman in coronets,
and military cousins,
There were captains by the hundred,
there were baronets by dozens.
Yet she heeded not their offers,

but dismissed them with a blessing;
Then she let down all her back hair
which had taken long in dressing.
Then she had convulsive sobbings
in her agitated throttle,
Then she wiped her pretty eyes
and smelt her pretty smelling-bottle.
So I whispered, 'Dear Elvira, say
what can the matter be with you?
Does anything you've eaten, darling Popsy,
disagree with you?'
But in spite of all I said,
her sobs grew more and more distressing,
And she tore her pretty back hair,
which had taken long in dressing.
Then she gazed upon the carpet,
at the ceiling then above me,
And she whispered, 'Ferdinando,
do you *really* really love me?'
'Love you?' said I, then I sighed
and then I gazed upon her sweetly —

For I think I do this sort of thing particularly neatly —
'Send me to the Arctic regions, or illimitable azure,
On a scientific goose-chase,
with my Coxwell or my Glaisher.
'Tell me whither I may hie me,
tell me, dear one, that I *may* know
Is it up the highest Andes?
Down a horrible volcano?'
But she said, 'It isn't polar bears,
or hot volcanic grottoes,
Only find out who it is that
writes those lovely cracker mottoes!'

II

'Tell me Henry Wadsworth, Alfred,
Poet Close, or Mister Tupper,
Do you write the bonbon mottoes
my Elvira pulls at supper?'
But Henry Wadsworth smiled,
and said he had not had that honour;
And Alfred, too, disclaimed the words

Peacock in a flask, from *Splendor Solis*, by
Salomon Trismosin, Germany, 1582

that told so much upon her.
'Mister Martin Tupper, Poet Close,
I beg of you inform us,'
But my question seemed to throw
them both into a rage enormous.
Mister Close expressed a wish that
he could only get anigh to me.
And Mister Martin Tupper sent
the following reply to me:
'A fool is bent upon a twig,
but wise men dread a bandit.'
Which I think must have been clever,
for I didn't understand it.
Seven weary years I wandered —
Patagonia, China, Norway,
Till at last I sank exhausted at
a pastrycook in his doorway.
There were fuchsias and geraniums,
and daffodils and myrtle,
So I entered, and I ordered
half a basin of mock turtle.
He was plump and he was chubby,

'Blackbirds in a Pie'. Illustration from 'Sing a Song of Sixpence'
R. Caldecott's Picture Book, G. Routledge & Son, London, 1879

he was smooth and he was rosy,
And his little wife was pretty, and particularly cosy.
And he chirped and sang, and skipped about,
and laughed with laughter hearty —
He was wonderfully active for so very stout a party.
And I said, 'Oh, gentle pieman,
why so very, very merry?
Is it purity of conscience,
or your one-and-seven sherry?'
But he answered, 'I'm so happy —
no profession could be dearer —
If I am not humming Tra! la! la!'
I'm singing Tirer, lirer!
'First I go and make the patties,
and the puddings and the jellies,
Then I make a sugar birdcage,
which upon a table swell is;
Then I polish all the silver,
which a supper-table lacquers;
Then I write the pretty mottoes
which you find inside the crackers' —
'Found at last!' I madly shouted.
'Gentle pieman, you astound me!'

Then I waved the turtle soup
enthusiastically round me.
And I shouted and I danced
until he'd quite a crowd around him —
And I rushed away exclaiming,
'I have found him! I have found him!'
And I heard the gentle pieman
in the road behind me trilling,
'Tira! lira! Stop him, stop him!
Tra! la! la! the soup's a shilling!'
But until I reached Elvira's house,
I never, never waited,
And Elvira to her Ferdinand's irrevocably mated!

W. S. GILBERT
The Bab Ballads

Variations Upon Whitebait

'Oh, yes, the whitebait,' rejoiced the Sphinx, glad of a subject to hide her emotion. 'Now tell me something nice about them, though the poor little things have long since disappeared. Tell me, for instance, how they get their beautiful little silver waterproofs?'

'Electric Light of the World,' I said, 'it is like this. While they are still quite young and full of dreams, their mother takes them out in picnic parties of a billion or so at a time to where the spring moon is shining, scattering silver from its purse of pearl far over the wide waters, silver, silver, for every little whitebait that cares to swim and pick it up.

'The mother, who has a contract with some such big restaurateur as ours here, chooses a convenient area of moonlight, and then at a given signal they all turn on their sides, and bask and bask in the rays, little fin pressed lovingly against little fin — for this is the happiest time in the young whitebait's life: it is at these silvering parties that matches are made and future consignments of whitebait arranged for. Well, night after night, they thus lie in the moonlight, first on one side then on the other, till by degrees, tiny scale by scale, they become completely lunar-plated. Ah! how sad they are until that happy time has to come.'

'And what happens to them after that?'

'One night when the moon is hidden, their mother comes to them with treacherous wile, and suggests they should go of on a holiday again to seek the moon — the moon that for a moment seems captured by the pearl-fishers of the sky. And so off they go merrily, but, alas, no moon appears, and presently they are aware of unwieldy bumping presences upon the surface of the sea, presences as of huge dolphins, and rough voices call across the water, till, scared, the little whitebaits turn home in flight — to find themselves somehow meshed in an invisible prison, a net as fine and strong as air...'

'What sad little lives! and what a cruel world it is!' said the Sphinx — as she crunched with her knife through the body of a lark, that but yesterday had been singing in the blue sky. Its spirit sang just above our heads as she ate, and the air was thick with the grey ghosts of all the whitebait she had eaten that night.

RICHARD LE GALLIENNE
The Yellow Book, VIII, January 1896

SUBTLE WIT

it is not the booze itself
that I regret so
much said the old brown
roach it is the
golden companionship of
the tavern myself
and my ancestors have been
chop house and tavern
roaches for hundreds of years
countless generations back
one of my elizabethan
forebears was plucked from
a can of ale in the

mermaid tavern by
will shakespeare and
put down kit marlowe's back
what subtle wits they were in
those days said i yes
he said and later
another one of my
ancestors was
introduced into a larded
hare that addison
was eating by dicky steele
my ancestor came
skurrying forth dicky
said is that your own
hare joe or a wig a
thing which addison
never forgave ...

DON MARQUIS
archy and mehitabel

Not Exactly a Square Meal

My dinner was brought, and four persons of quality, whom I remembered to have seen very near the king's person, did me the honour to dine with me. We had two courses, of three dishes each. In the first course, there was a shoulder of mutton, cut into an equilateral triangle, a piece of beef into a rhomboid, and a pudding into a cycloid. The second course was two ducks trussed up into the form of fiddles; sausages and puddings resembling flutes and hautboys, and a breast of veal in the shape of a harp. The servants cut bread into cones, cylinders, parallelograms and several other mathematical figures.

JONATHAN SWIFT
Gulliver's Travels

King Arthur and Guinevere at a banquet, with Sir Lancelot kneeling before them. From the *Romance of the Saint Graal*, by Robert De Borron, France, early 14th century

A la ueille de la penteci
ste qnt tout li compaig
non de la table ronde fu
rent uenu a camaelot et il orent
oi le seruice, il fisent mettre les ta

'Mushroom Monstrosities', by George Cruikshank,

published by *McLean's Monthly Sheet of Caricatures*, 1835

L'ART CULINAIRE CHEZ DIVERS PEUPLES. 6. Cuisine gigantesque d'un grand hôtel moderne.

LIFT

VÉRITABLE EXTRAIT DE VIANDE **LIEBIG.**

L'ART CULINAIRE CHEZ DIVERS PEUPLES. 1. Cuisine pompéienne au début de notre ère.

VÉRITABLE EXTRAIT DE VIANDE **LIEBIG.**

ONE WAY TO SERVE A MEAL

The few, that would give out themselves, to be
Court and town-stallions, and each-where, belye
Ladies, who are known most innocent, for them;
Those will I beg, to make me Eunuchs of;
And they shall fan me with ten Estrich tailes
A piece, made in a plume to gather wind.
We will be brave, Puffe, now we ha' the Med'cine,
My meat, shall all come in, in Indian shels,
Dishes of Agate, set in gold, and studded,
With Emeralds, Sapphyres, Hiacinths, and Rubies.
The tongues of Carpes, Dormise, and Camels heeles
Boil'd i' the spirit of Sol, and dissolu'd Pearle.

BEN JONSON
Sir Epicure Mammon in *The Alchemist*

L'Art Culinaire chez Diverses Peuples. Scenes from historical
kitchens were displayed on free cards when purchasing
tins or jars of Liebig Meat Extract in the 19th century

'For heaven's sake: say it's all right this time.'

GRAPES AND BOTTLES

I think wealth has lost much of its value,
if it have not wine.

RALPH WALDO EMERSON

KEATS ON CLARET

I like claret ... For really 'tis so fine — it fills one's mouth with a gushing freshness — then goes down cool and feverless — then you do not feel it quarrelling with your liver — no, it is rather a Peacemaker, and lies as quiet as it did in the grape; then it is as fragrant as the Queen Bee, and the more ethereal part of it mounts into the Brain, not assaulting the cerebral apartments like a bully in a badhouse looking for his trull, and hurrying from door to door bouncing against the wainscot, but rather walks like Aladdin about his enchanted palace so gently that you do not feel his step.

JOHN KEATS

Letter to George and Georgiana Keats in America, 18 February 1819

THE YEAR OF THE COMET

He then rang the bell, and having ordered two fresh glasses to be brought, he went out and presently returned with a small pint bottle, which he uncorked with his own hand; then sitting down he said, 'The wine that I bring here is port of eighteen hundred and eleven, the year of the comet, the best vintage on record. The wine which we have been drinking,' he added, 'is good, but not to be compared with this, which I never sell, and which I am chary of. When you have drunk some of it, I think you will own that I have conferred an obligation upon you.' He then filled the glasses, the wine which he poured out diffusing an aroma through the room; then motioning me to drink, he raised his own glass to his lips, saying, 'Come, friend, I drink to your success at Horncastle.'

GEORGE BORROW
The Romany Rye (1857)

Inscribed on a Pint-pot

There are several reasons for drinking
And one has just entered my head;
If a man cannot drink when he's living
How the Hell can he drink when he's dead?

Anon

Anacreontick Verse

Brisk methinks I am, and fine,
When I drink my capring wine:
Then to love I do encline,
When I drinke my wanton wine:
And I wish all maidens mine,
When I drinke my sprightly wine:
Well I sup, and well I dine,
When I drinke my frolick wine:
But I languish, lowre, and pine,
When I want my fragrant wine.

Robert Herrick

The Right Temperature

The Pergola tavern deserves its name, the courtyard being overhung with green vines and swelling clusters of grapes. The host is a canny old boy, up to any joke and any devilry, I should say. He had already taken a fancy to me on my first visit, for I cured his daughter, Vanda, of a raging toothache by the application of glycerine and carbolic acid.

We went into his cellar, a dim tunnel excavated out of the soft tufa, from whose darkest and chilliest recesses he drew forth a bottle of excellent wine — it might have lain on a glacier, so cold it was. How thoughtful of Providence to deposit this volcanic stuff within a stone's throw of your dining-table! Nobody need ice his wine at the Pergola.

Norman Douglas
Alone

Mistaken Identity

Did you ever taste Imperial Tokay? Your brother gave me some of the best ever tasted, I am told; and what do you think I said?

'Why, this cannot be Tokay!'

'Did you ever taste Tokay before?' said he.

'O yes, very often; but this is not Tokay.'

'Be pleased to tell me what it is, then,' quoth Lestock.

'I don't know; but not Tokay, or a different sort from what I ever tasted, for that was sour and always drunk in green glasses.'

Suddenly I recollected that I meant Hock!

MARIA EDGEWORTH
Letter to Mrs Edgeworth, 2 January 1841

'A Woman and Child by a Table', from *The Elegant Girl, or Virtuous Principles, the True Source of Elegant Manners*, published by S. Inman, London, 1817

But what a picture here is given?!
O Charity, meek child of Heaven?!
May all the rich thy virtues feel?;
And learn this lesson at each meal;
To clothe the naked, feed the poor;
Nor drive the beggar from their door.

Plate 5

THE COCKTAIL KING.

'The Cocktail King' by H. M. Bateman. From *Punch*, April, 1922

It Couldn't Have Been the Wine

The night Prince Aribert dined with his august nephew in the superb dining-room of the Royal apartments, Hans served, the dishes being brought to the door by other servants. Aribert found his nephew despondent and taciturn. On the previous day, when, after the futile interview with Sampson Levi, Prince Eugen had despairingly threatened to commit suicide, in such a manner as to make it 'look like an accident', Aribert had compelled him to give his word of honour not to do so.

'What wine will your Royal Highness take?' asked old Hans in his soothing tones, when the soup was served.

'Sherry,' was Prince Eugen's curt order.

'And Romanée-Conti afterwards?' said Hans. Aribert looked up quickly.

'No, not to-night. I'll try Sillery to-night,' said Prince Eugen.

'I think I'll have Romanée-Conti, Hans, after all,' he said, 'It suits me better than Champagne.'

The famous and unsurpassable Burgundy was served with the roast. Old Hans brought it tenderly in its wicker cradle, inserted the corkscrew with mathematical precision, and drew the cork, which he offered for his master's inspection. Eugen nodded, and told him to put it down.

Aribert watched with intense interest. He could not for an instant believe that Hans was not the very soul of fidelity, and yet, despite himself, Racksole's words had caused him a certain uneasiness. At that moment Prince Eugen murmured across the table.

'Aribert, I withdraw my promise. Observe that, I withdraw it.'

Aribert shook his head emphatically, without removing his gaze from Hans. The white-haired servant perfunctorily dusted his napkin round the neck of the bottle of Romanée-Conti, and poured out a glass. Aribert trembled from head to foot.

Eugen took up the glass and held it to the light.

'Don't drink it,' said Aribert very quietly. 'It is poisoned.'

'Poisoned!' exclaimed Prince Eugen.

'Poisoned, sire!' exclaimed old Hans, with an air of profound amazement and concern, and he seized the glass. 'Impossible, sire, I myself opened the bottle. No one else has touched it, and the cork was perfect.'

'I tell you it is poisoned,' Aribert repeated.

'Your Highness will pardon an old man,' said Hans, 'but to say that this wine is poison is to say that I am a murderer. I will prove to you that it is not poisoned. I will drink it.'

And he raised the glass to his trembling lips. In that moment Aribert saw that old Hans, at any rate, was not an accomplice of Jules. Springing up from his seat, he knocked the glass from the aged servitor's hands, and the fragments of it fell with a light tinkling crash partly on the table and partly on the floor.

The Prince and the servant gazed at one another in a distressing and terrible silence. There was a slight noise, and Aribert looked aside. He saw that Eugen's body had slipped forward limply over the left arm of his chair. The Prince's arms hung straight and lifeless; his eyes were closed; he was unconscious.

'Hans!' murmured Aribert. 'Hans! What is this?'

ARNOLD BENNETT
The Grand Babylon Hotel

JUST ANOTHER BOTTLE

The wine circulated languidly, and Mr Jorrocks in vain tried to get up a conversation on hunting. The Professor always started his stones or Mr Muleygrubs his law, varied by an occasional snore from Mr Slowman, who had to be nudged by Jones every time the bottle went round. Thus they battled on for about an hour.

'Would you like any more wine?' at length inquired Mr Muleygrubs, with a motion of rising.

'Not any more I'm obleged to you,' replied the obsequious Mr Jacob Jones, who was angling for the chaplaincy of Mr Marmaduke's approaching shrievalty.

'Just another bottle!' rejoined Mr Jorrocks encouragingly.

'Take a glass of claret,' replied Mr Muleygrubs, handing the jug to our master.

'Rayther not, thank ye,' replied Mr Jorrocks, 'not the stuff for me. By the way now, I should think,' continued Mr Jorrocks, with an air of sudden enlightenment, 'that some of those old ancient ancestors o' yours have been fond o' claret.'

'Why so?' replied Mr Muleygrubs pertly.

'Doesn't know,' replied Mr Jorrocks, musingly, 'but I never hears your name mentioned without thinking o' small claret. But come, let's have another bottle o' black strap — it's good strap — sound and strong — got wot I calls a good grib o' the gob.'

'Well,' said Mr Muleygrubs, getting up and ringing the bell, 'if you must, you must, but I should think you have had enough.'

'PORT WINE!' exclaimed he, with the air of a man with a dozen set out, to his figure footman, as he answered the bell.

ROBERT SMITH SURTEES
Handley Cross

MAGNUM OF DOUBLE-DIAMOND

'David,' said brother Ned.

'Sir,' replied the butler.

'A magnum of the double-diamond, David, to drink the health of Mr Linkinwater.'

Instantly, by a feat of dexterity, which was the admiration of all the company, and had been, annually, for some years past, the apoplectic butler, bringing his left hand from behind the small of his back, produced the bottle with the corkscrew already inserted, uncorked it at a jerk, and placed the magnum and the cork before his master with the dignity of conscious cleverness.

'Ha!' said brother Ned, first examining the cork and afterwards filling his glass, while the old butler looked complacently and amiably on, as if it were all his own property, but the company were quite welcome to make free with it. 'This looks well, David.'

'It ought to, sir,' replied David. 'You'd be troubled to find such a glass of wine as is our double-diamond and that Mr Linkinwater knows very well. That was laid down, when Mr Linkinwater first come, that wine was, gentlemen.'

'Nay, David, nay,' interposed brother Charles.

'I wrote the entry in the cellar-book myself, sir, if you please,' said David, in the tone of a man quite confident in the strength of his facts. 'Mr Linkinwater had only been here twenty year, sir, when that pipe of double-diamond was laid down.'

'David is quite right, brother Charles,' said Ned. 'Are the people here, David?'

'Outside the door, sir,' replied the butler.

'Show 'em in, David, show 'em in.'

At this bidding, the old butler placed before his master a small tray of clean glasses, and opening the door admitted the jolly porters and warehousemen whom Nicholas had seen below. They were four in all. As they came in, bowing and grinning, and blushing, the housekeeper, and cook, and housemaid, brought up the rear.

CHARLES DICKENS
Nicholas Nickleby

Rare Vintages and Vin Ordinaire

These are the children of long years of peace,
The high nobility of Earth's increase,
Superbly useless, set apart.
A symbol and epitome of art.
Not theirs the genial office to assuage
The labourer's thirst, but solely to engage
Sophisticated palates and invite
To feasts of intellectual delight.
In famous vineyards of the white or red
Meticulously tended, pruned and fed,
Gathered and pressed and to the vats conveyed
They wait in comfortable darkness laid
(Potential riches held in trust)
The gradual fermentation of the must,
Till, in due season grown authentic wine
By process scientific and divine,
Locked in their glassy cells they shall begin
The long novitiate of the château bin.
Raised to the priesthood each, an anchoret
Cloistered in crystal, lies imprisoned yet,
For not to such as these shall come the call
Till robed and hatted as a Cardinal.

But these are matters more than half divine.
Now let us praise the wine
That quenched the thirst of Chaucer, Rabelais,
Ronsard and Shakespeare, wine of every day
That warms the blood and strengthens talk and cheer
with wholesome draughts born of no boasted year,
Pressed in no vaunted vineyard, with no name
To catch the eye and set the thoughts aflame;
Of mere generic stock
Yet potent to unlock
The wagging tongue of Falstaff and entrance
The Spanish Knight of doleful countenance,
And wash the monstrous drought away
Of Patriarch Grangousier.
Let none of us contemptuously rebuff
Wine that was good enough
For men like these, but gladly sit and share
Our honest, rough, refreshing Ordinaire.

MARTIN ARMSTRONG
Wine and Food, 36

An Occasional Glass of Wine

MR CRANIUM. Pardon me: it is here — (*As he said these words, he produced a skull from his pocket, and placed it on the table, to the great surprise of the company.*) — This was the skull of Sir Christopher Wren. You observe this protuberance — (*The skull was handed round the table.*)

MR ESCOT. I contend that the original unsophisticated man was by no means constructive. He lived in the open air, under a tree.

THE REV. DOCTOR GASTER. The tree of life. Unquestionably. Till he had tasted the forbidden fruit.

MR JENKISON. At which period, probably, the organ of constructiveness was added to his anatomy, as a punishment for his transgression.

MR ESCOT. There could not have been a more severe one, since the propensity which has led him to building cities has proved the greatest curse of his existence.

SQUIRE HEADLONG — (*Taking the skull.*) *Memento mori.* Come, a bumper of Burgundy.

MR NIGHTSHADE. A very classical application, Squire Headlong. The Romans were in the practice of adhibiting skulls at their banquets, and sometimes little skeletons of silver, as a silent admonition to their guests to enjoy life while it lasted.

THE REVEREND DOCTOR GASTER. Sound doctrine, Mr Nightshade.

MR ESCOT. I question its soundness. The use of vinous spirit has a tremendous influence in the deterioration of the human race.

MR FOSTER. I fear, indeed, it operates as a considerable check to the progress of the species towards moral and intellection perfection. Yet many great men have been of opinion that it exalts the imagination, fires the genius, accelerates the flow of ideas, and imparts to dispositions naturally cold and deliberative that enthusiastic sublimation which is the source of greatness and energy...

MR JENKISON. I conceive the use of wine to be always pernicious in excess, but often useful in moderation: it certainly kills some, but it saves the lives of others. I find that an occasional glass, taken with judgment and caution, has a very salutary effect in maintaining that equilibrium of the system, which it is always my aim to preserve...

THOMAS LOVE PEACOCK
Headlong Hall

What's in a Name?

I trow there shall be an honest fellowship, save first
shall they of ale have new backbones. With strong ale
brewed in vats and tuns; Ping, Drangollie, and the
Draget fine, Mead, Mattebru, and the Metheling.
Red wine, the claret and the white, with Tent and
Alicant, in whom I delight. Wine of Languedoc and
of Orleans thereto; Single beer, and other that is
double; Spruce beer, and the beer of Hamburgh:
Malmsey, Tires, and Romany.

Colin Blobol's Testament
(15th century)

There was an Old Man with an Owl,
Who continued to bother and howl;
He sate on a rail,
And imbibed bitter ale,
Which refreshed that Old Man and his Owl.

Edward Lear

INDEX

ACKNOWLEDGEMENTS

The publishers and compiler of this anthology wish to thank the following individuals and firms for permission to quote material from the sources given:

Sheila Kaye-Smith courtesy of Mrs B Walthew; Gordon Catling, 'No Pie For Me, Please', The Society of Authors and Chatto & Windus; *Alone* and *Almanac*, both by Norman Douglas; 'Five Months at the Ice Station' by August Courtauld from *Northern Lights – the Official Account of the British Arctic Air-Route Expedition, 1930-1931*, Faber & Faber Ltd; *Hasta La Vista* by Christopher Morley, Jonathan Cape Ltd; *Eastern Approaches* by Fitzroy MacLean; Rosita Forbes, *The Secret of the Sahara*, Rupert Hart-Davis Ltd; *Trumpets from the Steep* by Diana Cooper; William Heinemann Ltd; *Venus in the Kitchen* by Pilaf Bey, edited by Norman Douglas, Longman; *South Latitude* by F. D. Ommanney, Macmillan & Co Ltd; 'Ferdinando and Elvira' from the *Bab Ballads* by Sir W. S. Gilbert, Methuen & Co Ltd; *What the World Showed Me* by Per Høst, Constable & Co; *Alone* by Admiral Richard Byrd, Faber & Faber Ltd; 'Subtle Wit' from *Archie & Mehitabel*; The Society of Authors and the Literary Trustees of Walter de la Mare; *In Defence of Drinking*, Nancy Spain, Hurst & Blackett Ltd; *Memoirs of William Hickey*, Vol IV, edited by Alfred Spencer; 'Avocado, or the Future of Eating' from *Crazy Like a Fox*, courtesy of The Estate of S J Perelman © 1944; 'A Meal in Abyssinia', pp. 94-5, from *When the Going was Good* by Evelyn Waugh (Duckworth 1946, Penguin Books 1976, 2003), © Evelyn Waugh, 1946; 'Guatemalan Food' from *Sing High! Sing Low!* by Sir Osbert Sitwell, Macmillan & Co Ltd.

We would also like to thank the International Wine and Food Society for the use of articles from their journals by André L Simon, Louis Golding, Ernest Oldmeadow, Betty P Metcalfe, Martin Armstrong, George Slocombe and Sir Francis Colchester-Wemyss.

NOTES ON THE ILLUSTRATIONS

The publishers owe their sincere thanks to the British Library for allowing reproduction of the following: *An Accomplished Lady's Delight in Cookery* (5951), page 15; *The Queen's Royal Cookery* (21817), pages 46 and 47; *An English Family at Table* (C.175b.44), page 51; *The Viceroy of Cantun* (9599), page 52; *Woman Sweetseller* (751), page 62; *Grainseller* (751), page 63; *Curry & Rice* (W2868), page 73; *Badhak or Qassab, The Caste of Butcher* (add.27255), page 92; *Bakers at Work* (NHIL 021 0000774), page 101; *Scene on an East Indiaman* (16555), page 102 and 103; *A Royal Ascetic* (2540), page 132; *A Javanese Grandee and Dutchman* (WD953), page 141; *Ghazi al din Haidar* (c.2185), page 142-3; *Pineapple* by George Brookshaw (2115) page 144; *Feasting and Dancing* (c.2192), page 171; *Dining at the Palais Royal* (NHIL 021 0000773), pages 182 and 183; *The Breakfast* (X42) page 194; *Pitt & Napoleon* (000828), page 203; *Richard II Dines with Dukes* (NHIL 0002337), pages 204-205; *Splendour Solis* (c.0448-01), page 215; *Blackbirds in a Pie* (8470), page 216; *King Arthur's Feast* (c.2185-05), page 225; *Sugar Making* (10 Album 52) page 255; *Onion and Cherry Tree* (11362.tif), page 256.

The publishers also wish to express their sincere thanks to Garwood & Voigt for kindly enabling us to reproduce the following original illustrations: 'Children Overindulging in Christmas Pudding', taken from *The Graphic* 1874; 'Henry' by Carl Anderson; 'A Very Rough Cruise', taken from *Punch* 1933; 'Gastronomic Symphony', *Punch* 1935; French menu; 'Rev. Dr Syntax and his Spouse', 1820; 'Mushroom Monstrosities' by George Cruikshank, 1835; *L'Art Culinaire chez Diverses Peuples*; and 'The Cocktail King', *Punch* 1992.

The illustration of Ernst Benary's 'Carrots' on page 113 is reproduced from *Album Benary*, published by G Severyns in 1876 and the illustration on page 57 is of Caxton's edition of Chaucer's *Canterbury Tales*, late 15th century. Jacket and End paper illustrations, plus illustrations on pages 33, 34, 44, 61, 64, 74, 83, 91, 104, 172 and 184 are taken from the original *Mrs Beeton's Book of Household Management* 1849 and *The Book of Family Cookery*, 1923. All Edward Lear illustrations to his limericks and poems are taken from the original *Book of Nonsense*, 1846. The James Thurber cartoon cartoon on page 10 is reproduced by kind permission of Rosemary Thurber.

Thanks are due to the following for permission to reproduce the following line drawings and cartoons: Aubrey Beardsley's illustration from *The Yellow Book* published between 1894 and 1897 by Bodley Head Ltd; W and A Gilbey Ltd, for two cartoons by Smilby from *The Compleat Imbiber*; Kingleo Studios and *What's On* for the Larry Cartoon; and *Punch* for the cartoons by Call, Larry, Sillince, Sprod and H F Wiles.

Nº 15   Process of boiling molasses in wate[r]
Bombay.   Vienna Exhi. Coll.

'Sugar Making'. Illustration of the process of boiling
molasses in water. Watercolour, c.1873

'Onion and Cherry Tree', depicting boys throwing down
cherries to a woman, Lombard, north Italy, c. 1440